Quayside Bristol

To our fellow Bristol Savages

QUAYSIDE
BRISTOL

THE CITY AND ITS PORT IN RECENT YEARS

FRANK SHIPSIDES & ROBERT WALL

Frank Shipsides —

Robert Wall.

REDCLIFFE
Bristol

First published in 1992 by
Redcliffe Press Ltd
49 Park St, Bristol.

© *Frank Shipsides and Robert Wall*

ISBN 1 872971 96 2

British Cataloguing-in-Publication Data.
A catalogue record for this book is available from the
British Library.

Typeset and printed by
The Longdunn Press Ltd, Bristol.

Contents

List of illustrations

Black & White

There are thirty-one pen and ink drawings throughout the book.

Credits

The author and artist are grateful to the many people who willingly gave their help in the preparation of this book and in particular the following:

From the Bristol Port Company: David Ord, Director, Commander Joe Bradley, Havenmaster and Julie Gough, Public Relations Department.

From the City of Bristol: Michael Robinson, Chief Executive, Martyn Heighton, Director of Leisure, Paul Elkin, Technical Curator, City Museum, John Williams, City Archivist and Jonathon Thorne and his staff of the Members Services Department.

From Avon County Council: The staff of the Central Reference Library for their never failing help and courtesy.

From Bristol's shipping industry in its many forms: Hubert Ashmead, Richard Goold Adams, Commander Tom Foden, John Hill, Richard Hill, Captain David Neill and Pilot Sam Vowles.

The Editor of *Ships Monthly*, Robert Shopland, gave advice from his great experience and the advice and help of the partners of Alexander Gallery, John Cleverdon, Jim Fardon, Alan Higgins and Peter Slade has been of great assistance. The patient guidance of our publisher, John Sansom was indispensable and without it this book would not have appeared.

Preface

It was in November 1981 that Frank Shipsides and I published *Bristol: Maritime City*, a general history of the port of Bristol and its affairs down the years since the city was founded in post-Roman times. That book has been long out of print and in the meantime another decade has been added to Bristol's history. These years climaxed in 1991 with the transfer of the port's operations to a private company after a century and a half of City Council control.

This latter event possibly closed a period of change in Bristol's maritime affairs which began as the Second World War ended. The theme of this book is the change that has occurred on and around Bristol's waterways since 1945. As the war ended and Bristol's maritime community emerged from a bloody and anxious time, the city was still the imperial trading port that had been created in the Victorian era. Unforeseen by all but a few, drastic and often traumatic change was at hand and the aftermath of the greatest change of all seems an appropriate time to update the history of the city and port.

In addition, there is a further opportunity to continue the study of the port of Bristol through the eyes and skill of Frank Shipsides who, in this book, adds another brilliant portfolio of paintings and drawings to enhance those already published by The Redcliffe Press. Again he has clearly expressed those characteristics of Bristol that so endear our city to those who live here.

Robert Wall
Bristol, November 1992

Bristol's war

"I also see . . . amid the ruins quiet, confident,
bright and smiling eyes, beaming with a
consciousness of being associated with a cause
far higher and wider than any human or
personal issue. I see the spirit of an unconquer-
able people."

*Winston S. Churchill, Prime Minister and
Chancellor of the University of Bristol,
speaking in Bristol, April 12th, 1941.*

In common with many other European cities, Bristol emerged from the
Second World War showing drastic physical and social changes. To seek the
origin of these, the researcher must go back to the war itself and the impact
that the fighting had on the old, rather self-satisfied society that dwelt in
Bristol in the decades to 1939.

There is no better starting point than Saturday, April 12th 1941. The
previous night, the City Docks had been the target for yet another raid by
Heinkel III bombers of the German Luftwaffe, based in Northern France.
Bristol's position as a port on the safer side of England for coastal shipping and
the great aircraft factories at Filton were the two reasons that made her a main
strategic target for the Germans. The first raid, although by a single bomber,
had come as early as June 18th 1940 with an attack on Filton and since then the
city had suffered a number of raids of increasing strength. These culminated in
six hours of destruction on the night of Sunday, November 24th/25th 1940
when Kesselring's II Luftflotte tore the heart out of old Bristol. Ostensibly
the target was the port at the centre of the city and hence the surrounding
areas, particularly around Bristol Bridge, succumbed to a hail of incendiaries
and high explosive bombs. Over a thousand of the latter were dropped on the
city and as dawn broke, some 200 people lay dead in the ruins and 700 were
undergoing treatment for injuries. 10,000 houses had been destroyed or
damaged and among the devastation, some of the best known buildings – the
Old Dutch House, St. Peter's Hospital, the Prince's Theatre and the Great
Hall of the University.

This raid of November 28th 1940 heralded the start of a campaign against

Bristol that was to last for months, the port being a constant target. Charles Hill's shipyard was hit again in the following raid on December 2nd, and part of the quayside at Welsh Back collapsed. Four nights later, six factories in the City Docks area were hit and Merchants Hall destroyed. The port stayed at work throughout the raids and ships continued to arrive and depart. King George VI toured the damaged areas on December 16th – a certain sign of government anxiety. The new year of 1941 opened with another sharp attack on the night of January 3rd/4th but, somewhat curiously, Avonmouth Docks were ignored until April 9th/10th, but the main dock installations escaped damage.

Two nights later came the attack on the city that was to be known as the 'Good Friday Raid'. At 2145 hours on April 11th, the mournful drone of the sirens again wailed out over the city. 150 aircraft hit areas as far apart as Portishead, Keynsham and Filton and thousands of incendiaries rattled down all across the city. In the usual pattern of Luftwaffe attacks these were followed up by two sessions of high explosive bombs. When the all-clear sounded at 0353 hours the following morning, 180 people lay dead and such diverse places as Horfield Rectory, Counterslip Tramway Power Station, the B.R.I., the Odeon and houses in Cotham Park had suffered heavy damage.

Into the chaos of the clearing and rescue operations of the early morning of Saturday, April 12th strode the formidable figure of the Prime Minister, with no one less than the Prime Minister of Australia and the American Ambassador in tow. Twelve years earlier, when the great statesman's fortunes were in decline, the University of Bristol, with commendable foresight, had made Winston Churchill its Chancellor. It was an honour of which he was immensely proud and he took the duties of the position very seriously. Hence he was in the city this day to fulfil a long-standing engagement to confer honorary degrees on Robert Menzies, the Anglophile Premier of Australia and also on John Winant, the successful and popular U.S. ambassador who had taken over from the anti-British Joe Kennedy.

Winston now set out on a tour of the damaged areas, taking both his guests and accompanied by Alderman Frank Parish, Chairman of Bristol's Emergency Committee and his Conservative Vice-Chairman Councillor Ken (later Sir Kenneth) Brown. The appearance of Churchill in the aftermath of an air raid on any city was a huge boost to morale, such was his popularity at the time, and so it proved in Bristol. Photographs of the occasion, transmitted by radio to New York, appeared in all the major American newspapers and Winant's presence alongside Churchill seemed to emphasise the then neutral U.S.A's commitment to the British cause.

When Churchill rose that afternoon in the spring of 1941 to speak to the University Congregation, with the smoking ruins around him, he was at his ebullient best. Clad in the black and gold robes of the Chancellor's office, he seemed the very embodiment of the city's defiance of Nazism.

> Here we are gathered in academic robes to go through a ceremonial and repeat formulas associated with the giving of university degrees. Many of those here today have been all night at their posts, and all have been under the fire of the enemy in long and protracted bombardment. That you should gather in this way is a mark of fortitude and phlegm, of a courage and detachment from material affairs worthy of all we have learned to believe of ancient Rome or modern Greece.
>
> I go about the country whenever I can escape for a few hours or for a day from my duty at headquarters, and I see the damage done by the enemy attacks; but I also see side by side with the devastation and amid the ruins quiet, confident, bright and smiling eyes, beaming with a consciousness of being associated with a cause far higher and wider than any human or personal issue. I see the spirit of an unconquerable people. I see a spirit bred in freedom, nursed in a tradition which has come down to us through the centuries, and which will surely at this moment, this turning point in the history of the world, enable us to bear our part in such a way that none of our race that come after us will have any reason to cast reproach upon their sires.

The 'Good Friday Raid' proved to be the last heavy assault on the city. True, the horror of the Broad Weir bus raid of August 28th 1942 had yet to come and there was the dying effort of the Luftwaffe in 1944 but by the summer of 1941 Bristol was over the worst. During the course of the war, the city endured 76 attacks and 1,299 Bristolians had died, with another 2,602 injured.

Some figures of the Port of Bristol's contribution to the cause of which Churchill spoke so eloquently will clearly illustrate the interest of the German High Command in the city. The quantity of trade entering the port in the year ending March 31st 1939 was 4,314,000 tons; in the year ending March 31st 1945, it had risen to 7,500,000 tons and the wartime yearly achievement averaged nearly 6,000,000 tons. Meanwhile, at Albion Dockyard, the shipyard of Charles Hill and Company had launched twenty six frigates, corvettes, boom defence vessels, landing craft and patrol boats for the Allied fleets.

Although here we are mainly concerned with maritime affairs, mention should be made of the war effort of Bristol's aircraft industry. The Bristol Aeroplane Company's plants at Filton and Patchway produced aircraft and aero-engines and were a key Luftwaffe target, as that force proved by a devastating raid on September 25th 1940. 160 bombs fell on the Filton factory, 72 people were killed and 166 injured of whom 19 were to die of their injuries.

Production was not held up for long, however, and the total achievement of Bristol's aviation industry was remarkable. Apart from producing the versatile Beaufighter which became one of the war's outstanding aircraft, the Bristol factories turned out 2,573 aircraft in Bristol itself and over 100,000 engines for such famous machines as the Wellington, Stirling, Halifax and Sunderland and many others. At the height of the war, employment in the Bristol factories alone soared to 30,000 plus.

The six years of the war at sea took a heavy toll of Bristol shipping and produced a lengthy casualty list of Bristol seamen. Bristol ships had fought the 1914–18 war at sea, on the oceans or in the far off Dardanelles. The 1939 war brought the conflict to Bristol's very doorstep as U-boats operated in the Bristol Channel and German aircraft were a common sight in west country skies. It was the U-boats that came first. With the war only two weeks old, U-29 struck west of Lundy, torpedoing and sinking the aircraft carrier H.M.S.*Courageous* with the loss of 514 lives. U-boats would maintain a constant presence in the Western Approaches and the entrance to the Bristol Channel throughout the entire war. Many Bristol based ships would fall victim to their attacks, while overhead was the ever present threat of the Luftwaffe. The first Bristol ship to be lost was the Bristol Steam Navigation's *Cato*, 710 grt, which went down off Minehead on March 3rd 1940, striking a mine laid by Lt. Otto Scuhart's U-29.

Typical of wartime activity was the story of the Bristol City Line's fleet of small liners which still sailed from the City Docks. *Toronto City*, 2500 grt, was on weather service duties in the North Atlantic when lost with all hands on July 1st 1941. The German navy made a particular effort to disperse these ships which were there to guide Allied aircraft across the Atlantic and *Toronto City* (Captain Garlick) was hunted down and sunk by U-108 (Lt. Cdmr Klaus Scholtze). *Montreal City*, 3066 grt, was lost to a torpedo from U-591 (Lt. Hansjurgen Zetsche) on December 21st 1942, when bad weather forced her convoy to scatter. Due to the ferocity of the gale, there were no survivors from Captain Chanter and his crew. On the night of May 5th 1943, *Bristol City*, 2864 grt, was hit by two torpedos from Lt. Rolf Manke's U-358 some 500 miles south east of Cape Farewell. The ship went down in nine minutes but Captain Webb and twenty-seven others were rescued by the corvette H.M.S. *Loosestrife.*

Another Bristol City Line ship, *Gloucester City*, 3071 grt, went to the aid of the survivors of the convoy attacked by the pocket battleship *Admiral Scheer* (Captain Kranke) on November 5th 1940, when the armed merchant cruiser *Jervis Bay* (Captain F. Fagen R.N.) heroically sacrificed herself to save her charges. In the southerly gale which blew that night, *Gloucester City* almost collided with a large warship heading due south that loomed up out of the mist and spray and passed within a few feet. Captain Smith always insisted that the ship could only have been the *Admiral Scheer*!

When the war ended in 1945, returning sailors found the port much the same as it had been in 1939. Also Bristol's main industrial installations were intact and little affected by the aerial bombardments. It was in the centre of the ancient city, among its Georgian houses, churches, shops, offices and public buildings that the air raid damage was most severe. The areas of Castle Street and Wine Street, and the great gap around the Horsefair north to Stokes Croft were all desolate, while there were many gaps in Park Street and the line stretching from Bristol Bridge south on both sides of Victoria Street to Temple Meads Station. The destruction of the central shopping areas meant that the suburban shopping streets of Bedminster and Gloucester Road enjoyed a boom for years after the war until the new shops in Broadmead opened.

Bristol now faced a challenging task of rebuilding the city and meeting the aspirations of the new generation that had grown up during the war and who had done much of the fighting. Not for them the stylised society of the thirties and they made this clear by returning a Labour Government with a working majority for the first time in the history of the party. So it was not surprising that Bristol's first post-war priority became a large new housing programme to alleviate the serious shortage caused by the war. The re-development, although planned, did not get going until 1950. Great new estates arose on the city boundaries at Hartcliffe, Withywood, Bishopsworth, Lockleaze, Henbury and Lawrence Weston. Whereas houses arose in their thousands, the amenities that turn estates into communities were often not forthcoming and even today many are lacking. Additionally, even if progress was made in the suburbs, where 23,000 new school places were provided by 1963, redevelopment of the central areas was woefully slow and often controversial, particularly over issues raised in the City Docks. How these great issues were handled is a central theme of later chapters of this book.

The other great challenge faced by Bristol in the post war years was the modernisation of its now ageing port. At Avonmouth and the City Docks trade fell off somewhat as the war ended. Great Britain had exhausted herself with the war and was near bankrupt, so the impetus of the post-war export drive with its emphasis on dollar earning drove the figures upward once more. Bristol still looked westward to North America, and thousands of Midland built motor vehicles went out through Avonmouth to Canada and the U.S.A. By 1951, trade had reached its wartime level of 5.5 million tons and it would rise to 7.7 million by 1961.

Charles Hill's *Boston City*.

While the port prospered in these years, it was not difficult to see that change was imminent. The last visit of a large commercial sailing vessel to Avonmouth took place with the arrival of the four-masted barque *Passat* on October 12th 1947, with a cargo of wheat from Australia. She had made the passage in 143 days. Other more radical changes lay ahead for the port, although they were someway off. Most of Bristol's trade was carried in small tramps and liners, mostly not larger than 8,000 tons, and the immediate post-war years saw a boom in the building of these as companies replaced their war losses. There was also a need for new ancilliary craft and Albion Dockyard was busy with new orders, mainly with craft built for special purposes. Typical were a Trinity House light and buoy tender, a lightship for Ireland, numerous dredging craft and a variety of tugs from small harbour vessels to large ocean going salvage ships.

Those in the shipping industry with foresight had long argued the case for larger ships. One can trace the birth of this thesis as far back as Brunel and now, as the 1950s dawned, the technology was on hand and shipyards, in Japan in particular, strove to cut both production times and costs per ton. British shipyards, riddled with long established restrictive practices, never fully learnt the lesson of changes in ship design and cargo handling that now began to appear. The super-tanker was a creature of the fifties and she was followed by the large bulk carrier and the container ship. Only a few people in Britain realised that a maritime revolution was at hand, but amongst these were the few senior councillors and officials that made up the Port of Bristol Authority in its headquarters in Queen's Square.

Long before the war even, the P.B.A. had a policy which envisaged port expansion and for years they had quietly bought up any land which came on the market at the mouth of the Avon on the south bank of the river opposite Avonmouth Docks. By the mid-fifties, almost the entire site needed for a new 40 berth super-port was available at Portbury and initial schemes were being prepared.

The Second World War, therefore, created two especial challenges for Bristol and its port and people. Although they did not realise it at the time, the solutions to these problems were to take the better part of half a century, be the generators of much bitter controversy and create further problems which persist to this day. When the author arrived in Bristol on September 17th 1947 to start a Bristol Aeroplane Company engineering apprenticeship, the arguments were just beginning. Proposals for the rebuilding of Bristol had been under discussion as early as May 1941 and a report to the City Council in July of that year was already talking about the need for an inner circuit road

Elder & Fyffe's *Ariguani*.

and a bus station! There were also the first efforts at conservation in a list of central area buildings which were considered worthy of retention. There was nothing much new in all this compared with pre-war plans but the 1944 plan introduced two ideas which eventually found their way into (partial) realisation – a large university precinct and the transfer of the main shopping area from Wine Street to Broadmead. The plan was submitted to the Government in March 1946 (only Plymouth was ahead of Bristol) and was severely curtailed in Ministerial responses in December of that year and in June 1947, prompted in some degree by local opposition led by the Chamber of Commerce and other groups. The fight was on and its results are set out in the account that lies ahead.

The making of a modern port

"The old spirit of enterprise began to reassert itself. Many things were done to bring the port up to modern requirements. No doubt municipal control, with its 'multitude of counsellors', often hindered progress."

Charles Wells August, 1909.

To the servicemen and women who returned to Bristol after five and a half years of war, the port of Bristol in 1945 looked much the same as they had last seen it in 1939. True, the scars of war were all around to see but the busy self-confident life of the dockside was as vibrant as ever. Coasters called in at the City Docks again, and cargoes came and went from Canon's Marsh, Welsh Back, Wapping and Prince's Wharf. The Scandinavian timber boats were back at Baltic Wharf and *Boston City* and her sisters were alongside A Shed.

Charles Hill's yard at Albion Dockyard were busy on an order book which included a big paddler for Campbells, coasters for the Bristol Steam Navigation Company, a tender for Trinity House, lightships, numerous dredging craft for the P.B.A. and a variety of tugs from small harbour to large ocean going salvage types.

The fifties were prosperous ones for the Port Authority. It was profitable and, for the first time in generations the port operation was not subsidised by the ratepayers. Such commercial success was the background to the changes which now came onto the maritime scene. The Docks Committee were clearly correct in their view that merchant ships would get larger but there is little evidence to show that they understood the changes in the types of trade that Bristol would be expected to handle by the end of the century. Their proposals for the new dock at Portbury, therefore, had adequate size for all but the very largest ships, but in terms of cargo handling and hinterland facilities, it might have belonged to the 1930s in the same way that the Broadmead shopping centre was the creature of the pre-war ideas for perfect shopping.

To illustrate the manner in which the post-war changes happened, there is no better example than the history of Bristol's shipping companies. The Bristol City Line, owned by Charles Hill and Sons, was typical of many family-owned

21

liner companies in the British Mercantile Marine, which in 1939 at the outbreak of war numbered 8,977 ships over 100 tons, grossing a staggering 21,000,000 tons of shipping! Smaller companies operating were Bristol Steam Navigation, Alfred Duggan's Ald Shipping, Whitwill (Shipping) Ltd, Osborne and Wallis and other firms, while there was a strong sand and gravel trade.

Prior to the war, all the Bristol City Line's ships were of such a size as to allow them to pass up the river to the City Docks. By 1945, half the fleet had been lost and only three elderly ships – *New York City* (1917), *Gloucester City* (1919) and *Boston City* (1920) were available to restart the Atlantic trade from Canon's Marsh. The latter ship was something of a Bristol favourite, being the last Bristol City liner to be built at Albion Dockyard and that as far back as 1920. In the event, she was also the last City liner to use the City Docks, making her last trip there in February 1951, after which she was sold to Italian owners and broken up in 1960. Additional tonnage was needed and this was acquired using wartime built tonnage or ex-enemy vessels which were then coming on the market.

The first ship to be acquired was the *Fairmount Park*, 7502 grt, which was bought in 1946 and renamed *Montreal City* in the customary nomenclature of the company. This was followed in 1948 by *Bristol City* and *Wells City*, the latter a prize that started life as a Hamburg-America cargo liner in 1922 and was captured by the cruiser H.M.S. *Delhi* on October 25th 1939. *Birmingham City* (1950) and *New York City* (1951) were further additions and *London City* was chartered for a few months in 1951. All these ships were too big to get up the river to Bristol and Hill's main terminus now became 'S' Shed at Avonmouth. Here they hoped to operate with their own docker force as they had done for many years at Canon's Marsh. This meant that they were ensured a rapid and regular turn round. However, this practice was not in the rule-book at Avonmouth and the stevedores would have nothing to do with it. These restrictive practices were to badly handicap the British port industry for decades and Avonmouth suffered its full share. Not until the mid-eighties when the dock labour scheme was abolished would British ports be free of this well-meaning but debilitating handicap.

As the larger ships joined the fleet, the small pre-war vessels were sold – *Gloucester City* and *Boston City* in 1951, *New York City* the previous year. This post-war policy seems to have been quite successful for Hills and it is clearly no coincidence that their commercial progress occurred at the same time as considerable tonnage increases were handled by the P.B.A. In his history of the company *Shipshape and Bristol Fashion* (Redcliffe Press rev. ed. 1983), John Hill says that this profitable trading in the mid-fifties allowed

Tug: *Ernest Brown*.

Hills the freedom to order their first new building since the *Boston City* in 1920. They went to the Readhead Yard in Sunderland for three ships, all of five and a half thousand tons or so and these were delivered as *Gloucester City* (1954), *New York City* (1956) and *Bristol City* (1959). With the advantage of hindsight, it is difficult to see the reasoning behind the decision to build these three ships with steam turbine machinery. By this time diesel engines were becoming standard for this type of ship. John Hill explains that at the time the firm had an Engineering Superintendent who had long experience of steam and this officer persuaded the chairman, Charles Hill, to stick with steam. As the new build ships were delivered the secondhand tonnage bought in the post-war years was sold off.

This building and selling was fairly typical practice among cargo liner companies of the period and Hills found themselves up against formidable competition at Avonmouth from the big names of the business like Cunard and Donaldson. In 1959, the St. Lawrence Seaway opened and ocean going ships were given access to the whole Great Lakes system. Hills *Toronto City* was the first British ship to reach Milwaukee in the season that the last locks on the system were completed. The new routes did not prove profitable, however, owing to the enormous increase in distance to be run at the same freight rates. In 1961, the Lord Mayor, Alderman Charles Smith travelled to Toronto, the

23

city of his birth for a civic visit on board *Birmingham City*, together with Charles Worth, Chairman of the Port Authority and John Hill who was President of the Chamber of Commerce in that year. The visit attracted considerable publicity to the docks and shipping services.

The need for higher speed and capacity led Hills in 1963 to order two motorships, the first diesel driven in the history of the company. These were built by Burntisland and emerged as *Montreal City* and *Halifax City*. They were the first large Bristol-owned motorships. Already the shipping revolution, particularly in container traffic, was in full swing and these years coincided with the continuing opposition of the Government to the building of Portbury Dock. The future for the container trade at Bristol looked bleak and Hills did not proceed with plans to build container ships of their own. Rather they looked around for partners and found one in the Bibby Line of Liverpool, one of Britain's longest established and famous liner companies. Derek Bibby chartered two further motorships to Hills, the Doxford built *Coventry City* and *Toronto City* which arrived at Avonmouth for service in 1966. Once again older tonnage was sold off and the company now had four modern motorships with which to maintain the North Atlantic services. In the event this modernisation proved to be too late.

Mr. Charles Hill, the fourth bearer of the name, retired in 1968 and was succeeded as chairman by his son Richard. Richard Hill is one of the most significant figures in Bristol maritime history in the second half of the twentieth century and he was now to carry on a valiant fight to retain shipping and shipbuilding industries in Bristol, in which he did not always get the support he deserved. To meet the container revolution head on, in partnership with Bibby and Cie Maritime Belge, he formed Dart Container Line, which planned to operate three big container vessels between Antwerp, Southampton, Halifax, Nova Scotia, New York and Norfolk, Virginia. Bristol City Line's contribution to this was the 31,000 ton *Dart Atlantic*, a 21 knot giant built with Government aid at the Swan Hunter yard on the Tyne.

The Dart line started auspiciously but severe competition and US Government preferential policies proved too heavy a financial burden for Hill's parent company and in February 1972 Bibby bought a controlling interest in the line, to be followed by total acquisition of the shares in the following November. It was the end of a transatlantic line which had operated from Bristol since the first *Bristol City* had sailed from the port in 1879. Nevertheless, the building of *Dart Atlantic* was a significant achievement. She was the largest and fastest ship to appear on the Bristol register at the time and the largest British container ship up to the time of her launch, costing £7

24

million to build. After the sale of Bristol City Line to Bibby, the latter disposed of *Dart Atlantic* in 1980 to C.Y. Tung, the great Hong Kong shipping magnate, who leased her to Canadian Pacific. Ironically, she had been back on the routes for which Hills intended her.

The saga of the Bristol City Line illustrates the dilemma facing shipowners in the post-war years. This dilemma also faced the port authorities and nowhere more than in Bristol. Bristol had been the largest municipally owned port in Britain since the middle of the nineteenth century and any financial investment by the Docks Committee was carefully watched by anxious ratepayers. As we have seen, the Docks Committee started buying land south of the Avon in the 1920s, rightly judging that the size of ships would grow beyond the limits of its dock entrances. By the early 1950s, they were ready to proceed, all the necessary land being available with the exception of a residential camp site at Sheephouse Farm, which was not a great handicap to the project. The initial schemes for the Portbury Dock were drawn up and when these were published in 1960, it was fairly clear that the 40 berth super-port proposed was far too ambitious. The Ministry of Transport were not prepared to authorise the scheme in that form, although it did indicate that a modified scheme would receive sympathetic consideration. Although the Docks Committee members did not realise it at the time, it would take ten years of bitter controversy between Bristol and Whitehall before the necessary government approval was obtained for port expansion in Bristol.

There were two elements to the opposition to Bristol. One was the lobby mounted at Westminster by Welsh MPs on behalf of the South Wales ports which stretch on the north side of the Bristol Channel from Milford Haven in the west to Newport in the east. At the time that Bristol put forward its plans, the South Wales ports were in the early stages of a long decline. They had long existed on the export of coal, a trade that was now ending and their handling gear and infrastructure was in need of expensive restoration. Only Milford Haven with its oil terminal and Port Talbot with iron ore could point to a certain future and the Welsh ports saw Bristol as a modern port on the estuary which would drive them out of existence. The second element was the opposition of other major ports like Liverpool and London, and to some degree Southampton. All these already handled larger ships such as those that Bristol proposed to take, and to a degree felt threatened by her plans. This was readily understood in Bristol but the Welsh stand was derided as another ploy by the old enemy. Bristol quickly pointed out that, although the Welsh ports were offering outright objection to the Bristol scheme, nowhere in South Wales was there a port that was prepared to put up money to build a single new lock entrance to handle larger ships. Nevertheless, the controversy ensured that a large body of Welsh MPs were on hand to oppose at Westminster any bill promoted by the Port of Bristol Authority.

The Docks Committee had, in the meantime, gone back to the drawing board and in early 1964 they produced a much modified plan with a water area of seventy acres. This looked a far more feasible suggestion, based on construction costs of a modest £14 million. Now the politicians began to take a hand and, as it turned out, their influence would have a crucial impact. Not long after Bristol's plans were resubmitted to the Department of Transport, the Labour Government of Harold Wilson took office in October 1964. With several Welsh MPs in the Cabinet, not the least of whom was Jim Callaghan who represented the area which contained Cardiff Docks, it went without saying that the Welsh lobby was certain to be more effective. Confidence in the Portbury scheme nevertheless remained high in Bristol and it came as a severe shock when, in a Government White Paper on transport in 1966, the Secretary of State, Richard Marsh turned down Bristol's proposal. The Minister argued that the P.B.A. had not calculated the data in its forecasts on prudent economic grounds and said he did not believe the new dock would ever be profitable. All Bristol suspected that the Welsh lobby had much to do with the Government's decision.

The arguments flew backwards and forwards between London, Cardiff and Bristol. When the author joined the Docks Committee in May 1967, the way ahead at Portbury was the sole preoccupation. In those days, the committee was largely made up of people who had spent a lifetime in the Bristol shipping industry. They came from both sides of the political divide and were united in their all out effort to win acceptance of Bristol's proposals. Bert Peglar, Arthur Parish and Jack Fisk from Labour, Sir Kenneth Brown, Alfred Duggan and Leonard Stevenson from the Citizen (Conservative) Party continued to press the case at every opportunity but the Government remained unmoved.

The breakthrough came in 1969 when politics once again took a hand. In a letter to the *Western Daily Press*, the leader of the Opposition, Edward Heath, told editor Eric Price that any future Conservative ministry of his would give permission for West Dock, as the plan was now called, but only on the understanding that the City of Bristol raise the costs of the project and that there would be no Government subsidy of any kind. A year later, in June 1970, when he entered No. 10 as Prime Minister, Ted Heath was as good as his word and the Bristol West Dock Bill started its parliamentary progress in January 1971. The second reading was on a cold February evening. Several members of the committee, including the Chairman, Ted Wright, Arthur Parish and the author were in the Commons chamber to witness the debate. The Bristol case

The Cumberland Basin, as it was about 1950.

was brilliantly argued by Tony Benn who sat for Bristol South-East in those days but he was faced by a barrage of vocal opposition from Welsh members. Exactly on the stroke of ten, the passage of the bill was moved by Robert Cooke, MP for Bristol West, who had organised a sufficient tally of his Conservative colleagues to get the measure through. On the way home to Bristol, the Docks Committee Party celebrated the victory in a lay-by off the A4 with several bottles of champagne, brought along for the purpose. The Bristol West Dock Act received the Royal Assent on July 27th 1971. Work on the site was inaugurated in April 1972 by the Minister of Transport, the Yeovil MP John Peyton, with a completion target date of 1975.

The new dock provided for ships up to 75,000 tonnes carrying capacity. The water area is 70 acres and the planned dredged depth of water 45 feet. Three quays each provide 2,000 feet of berthing and the entrance lock measures 1,200 feet long by 140 feet wide. It is the largest of its kind in Britain. As this new dock began to take shape, other forces were already gathering which would have a dramatic and almost disastrous impact on the project's early years. The problem lay with the financing of the project. At this time the port made no demand on the ratepayer but this was soon to change. The original estimate of £14 million was to be funded by borrowing and 'rolling up' the interest charges

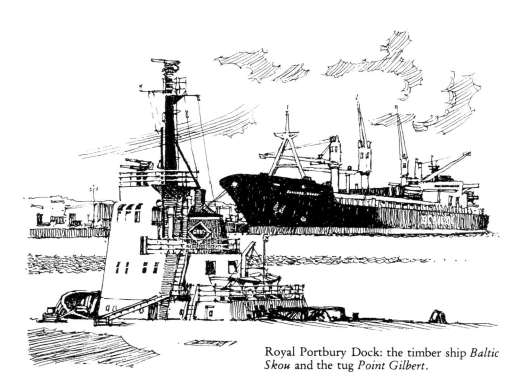

Royal Portbury Dock: the timber ship *Baltic Skou* and the tug *Point Gilbert*.

thus accumulated into the total cost of the project. The capital borrowing would then be supported by the trading profit from the dock. Two major events upset this comfortable plan. First in 1973, as Bristol celebrated 600 years as a county (a status granted in a Charter of Edward III) the 1972 Local Government Act came into force, reducing the City Council to district status and creating the County Council of Avon. This legislation greatly reduced Bristol's financial power as a local authority. And then, just at a time when stable prices were critical to West Dock construction costs, in October 1973, the Yom Kippur War broke out in the Middle East, the result of which was to send world oil prices soaring and initiating a round of world-wide inflation which would not subside until 1980.

The result of all this was that when Queen Elizabeth II arrived in HMY *Britannia* on August 8th 1977 to open Royal Portbury Dock, a name she chose herself, the total costs of the dock had risen to £52 million and Bristol had collected a financial burden which it was ill prepared to carry. The inevitable consequence was a large subsidy from the ratepayers which in some years in the seventies rose to £17 million annually. In his speech of welcome to Her Majesty

28

The sand hopper *Badminton* on Redcliffe Backs.

The Merchant Venturers' Hall, Clifton.

that August day of 1977, the Lord Mayor of Bristol, E. J. (Ted) Wright said that on that day 'Bristol comes to the end of the beginning.' To those charged with running the new dock, the beginning was anything but propitious, but five years were to pass before any action was taken to relieve the situation.

In May 1983, the author formed a minority Conservative administration in Bristol City Council following the elections held that month. He and his colleagues determined that the debt load must be removed, and with the approval of H.M. Treasury, raised a bond with the Trustee Savings Bank to borrow £50 million to pay off the docks debt on Portbury and to redeem the bond by selling off surplus council property over the next few years. With the support of the Liberals, this scheme was put through council and proceeded successfully until 1986. The Labour Group was back in overall control by then and they rearranged the loan over a much longer period. This had the effect of placing the load back on the local taxpayer and matters stood that way until in 1990 the city received a proposal to take over the port from a group from the private sector.

The story of that bid and the events that transpired from it is told in the closing chapter of this book.

The *Favell*: the last sailing ship built by Charles Hill.

I

The waterfront, early 1950s.
II

Welsh Back, around 1960.
III

A reminder of the Golden Age: the *Viking* passing Pill in the
early part of the century.

IV

The Port of Bristol Offices: Queen Square in the 1970s.

V

The *Lord Nelson* on a recent visit.
VI

The *Bristol Queen* in the Channel.
VII

An autumn evening: The *Marques* and the *Inca*.
VIII

Concrete and conflict

"There are only two things that matter in planning – money and land. That's all you need to know".

Alderman W.H. Hennessy,
Chairman of the Planning &
Public Works Committee, to the
author when the latter joined the
committee in May 1960.

To the visitor to Bristol who desires a five minute object lesson in the post-war history of the City Docks and the centre of the city, there is no better place to start than the south end of Prince Street bridge. For Bristol this is holy ground, for Brunel's *Great Western* was launched just across the quay at Wapping on July 19th 1837. Immediately across the road at Prince's Wharf stand L and M Sheds, rebuilt in 1951 as the most modern in the City Docks to replace Prince's Shed demolished by the Luftwaffe in 1941. Today the cargoes have gone and the sheds house the city's Industrial Museum. Behind one, the concrete towers around the city centre, largely put up in the sixties, block off the old skyline of city churches, while across the water, the squat half complete Lloyds Bank development dominates Canon's Marsh. The best that can be said of its appearance is that it looks better than the three 1920s tobacco bonds that were demolished to make way for it. Opposite, at Narrow Quay, the Bush Warehouse, built in the 1830s for the tea trade now houses the successful Arnolfini project.

Immediately ahead to the left there rises a red-brick apartment building. This is Merchants House, built in 1981 as part of the Merchants Landing housing scheme, and designed by the Ronald Toone Partnership. The irony is that this modern housing block is built on the site where the offices of the Bristol Steam Navigation Company stood. BSN as we shall call it, was Bristol's oldest surviving steamship company and its post-war history is typical of the fate of the short sea traders, just as that of Charles Hill typified the liner trades.

A host of small coasting companies used the City Docks in their heyday and many of the ships were familiar sights to Bristolians. Even in Liverpool and the

New building in the city docks: Merchants' Landing.

Pool of London the quaysides were not so accessible to everyday life as they were in Bristol. Alongside U and V Sheds (now the Exhibition Centre) the ships of Coast Lines and William Sloan of Glasgow were easy to spot from the top of a Brislington bus as it made its way round the Tramway Centre. Other well known shipowners using Bristol were the General Steam Navigation Company whose origins went back to the eighteenth century and who were based on the Thames, as were F. T. Everard & Sons Ltd. who remain in business today. Then there were J. Lauritzen from Denmark, the Bratt boats with timber from Sweden, N.V. Hollandsche Stoom (Holland Steamship Co.) and Bugsier Reederei from Germany which ran a regular service to Hamburg and Bremen until well into the sixties.

The origins of the BSN go back to the earliest steamers to operate services on the Bristol Channel. The first steamship to offer commercial sailing out of the city to sea (as opposed to canals) was the p.s. *Britannia*, built in 1816 for the Holyhead-Ireland service, which visited Bristol in April 1817 under the command of Lt. Robert Wall, R.N.! While the local press were enthusiastic about the *Britannia*, she did not cause local shipowners to place immediate orders for steamships. It was five years later that, in April 1822, the War Office Steam Packet Company placed a steamship, the *George IV*, in regular service between Bristol and Cork. The title of the company is misleading as it was entirely in private hands. In 1827 it became the General Steam Packet Company and then through several further name changes until it became the Bristol Steam Navigation Company in 1871. In 1836 the terminal for the Irish service was moved to Dublin and the company continued to run this until it ceased trading in 1980. After the war, they restarted the services to Antwerp and Rotterdam and were regular customers at Albion Dockyard for modern tonnage. In 1949/50 came *Pluto* and *Juno*, then in 1953/54 *Apollo* and *Milo*. The brand new *Apollo* was chosen to be one of the merchant ships present at the June 1953 Coronation Review of the Fleet by the newly-crowned Queen Elizabeth II. In 1957 came the *Echo*. Then, as if in stubborn defiance of commercial omens which were already unpropitious, two very modern vessels came out in 1963 called *Dido* and *Hero*.

It was a ship of the BSN Company that was involved in one of the very few major accidents to post-war Bristol shipping. On April 24th 1963, the company's coaster *Cato* was lying at P Shed at Avonmouth when she was rammed amidships by the Ellerman liner *City of Brooklyn*. What should have been a normal docking became a nightmare when the *City of Brooklyn*'s engines failed to respond to an order to go astern at a vital moment and the big ship almost cut the *Cato* in half. She went straight to the bottom of the dock but the crew scrambled ashore. The *Cato* was raised later by T. R. Brown and Sons. The head of Browns, Sir Kenneth Brown, took a great deal of personal interest in the salvage operations and gave the author a weekly update as we sat next to each other in Bristol's Planning Committee meetings. Browns temporarily patched *Cato*, pumped her out and towed her to Newport for scrap as she had been declared a constructive total loss. The *Cato* had an unfortunate history as six years earlier, in 1957, she had run down and sunk off Portishead the tug *Sea Prince*, owned by C.J. King and Sons.

The last years of the BSN operations in Bristol were a brave struggle to fight off the inevitable as the Irish and short-sea continental trades moved into containers and lorries carried on ro-ro vessels on the cross channel routes. Led by the late Douglas Lovell, who was a prominent Conservative Chairman in the city, it developed its own container berth for the Irish trade at N Shed at Avonmouth. Several ships were converted to carry containers and this trade continued after the closure of the City Docks. It finally closed in 1980.

Of the other lines trading into Bristol City Docks Coast Lines Ltd must be mentioned. Its familiar black funnel with a white chevron once decorated the largest fleet of coasters in the world. Some of its ships had provision for a dozen or so passengers and it was their proud boast that no port in the British Isles was out of reach of their ships. Their main route from Bristol was to Belfast which they usually operated from T Shed, Canon's Marsh. T Shed was demolished in the seventies and the site now used as a car park for the *Lochiel*, an ex- Macbrayne island motor vessel now used as a floating pub. Another well known company to use T Shed was William Sloan of Glasgow who first started running into Bristol from their home port in 1858. Using only 3 or 4 ships at any one time, they had a reputation for the longevity of their vessels which quite often lasted for half a century in the company's service. The final service from Glasgow was made by the *Kelvin* in May 1965 after which Sloans operated from Belfast. Since 1958, the business had been wholly owned by Coast Lines and when they closed the Belfast service in 1968, the Sloan line went out of existence.

In addition to British owned ships, many foreign vessels used Bristol. Typical was Adolph Bratt of Gothenberg in Sweden. This family firm had owned ships since 1890 and came to Bristol first in the 1920s. Their main cargo was timber, a long term Bristol import from Scandinavia that dates back to the Middle Ages. A large area of the south-east side of the docks at Baltic Wharf was used exclusively for timber imports from the 1850s onwards and it was here that the Scandinavian ships discharged their cargoes. But the trade eventually dribbled away and was replaced by package timber imported in huge quantities from North America in the early years of Royal Portbury Dock. When the City Docks closed to merchant shipping, the empty space at Baltic Wharf lay sterile for a decade.

On and around the "ocean-going" quays, there flourished other trades. Woodpulp and paper discharged at Avonmouth or Bristol was taken in barges and lighters up the Feeder Canal to the paper mills at St. Annes. Tobacco was also carried up from Avonmouth in this manner. Small tugs with a group of barges in tow were a frequent sight, carrying the house colours of Ashmeads and Browns. Then there were specialist vessels like the colliers of Osborn & Wallis and the sand sucking dredgers of the Bristol Sand & Gravel Company, operated by the Peters family and the Holms Sand and Gravel Company, which was run in keen but friendly rivalry by the Browns.

It was the trade to Scandinavia and continental ports like Rotterdam that occupied the City Docks in the last decade of commercial operations. But by the end of that decade, in 1970, the coastal trade went largely by road, crossing to the continent in roll-on, roll-off ferries and bringing work in full measure to east coast and channel ports which grew even more with Britain's membership of the EEC. General cargo and even such traditional Avonmouth cargoes as New Zealand frozen lamb began to be containerised and one large container ship might carry five times as much as a traditional freighter. The time had come for change, which was overdue in fact, and the changes shook Bristol to her foundations, provoked public controversies that bid to outdo those of the nineteenth century and left behind problems, many of which still await final solution.

By 1970, the City Docks were losing £200,000 a year. The scale of the decline can be judged by the figures for June 1963 when eighty ships berthed in the docks as compared with October 1969 when only twenty eight arrivals were recorded. In 1969 also, the long established Bristol Steam Navigation's direct service to Rotterdam was withdrawn as it was no longer profitable. As we have seen, Coast Lines had closed earlier in 1968 and the foreign flag vessels, particularly those from the Netherlands, had all but disappeared from the Avon. To all this the Port of Bristol Authority (which meant in effect the City Council) had a clear strategy as far as its port operations were concerned. The first objective, as we have seen and which eventually succeeded, was the building of Portbury Dock to make Bristol available to all but the very largest merchant ships. The second part of the strategy consisted of no less a proposal than the closure of the City Docks to commercial shipping, so ending trades that were established when the Normans occupied Bristol in the first century A.D. In the event the decision to close the docks did not surprise the average

Freeland Place, Hotwells overlooking the Avon.

Bristolian. The signs of commercial decay were there for all to see. What caused hackles to rise was the plan offered by the city planners for the future use of the disued waterways. To understand the reasons for the public outcry one must go back to the origins of Bristol's post-war planning strategy and its impact on the city up to that time in 1969.

For the first quarter century after the war, Bristol persisted in administering its planning policies through the City Engineer whose official title was 'City Engineer and Planning Officer'. At that point, the function divided and ran as two departments – engineering and planning. In many ways the system had practical advantages, because the City Engineer also acted as City Surveyor and, importantly, Highways Officer. Many critics, mostly with the benefit of hindsight, have quoted this arrangement as the cause of many of Bristol's planning mistakes in these years. While there may be some substance in this argument, it must be said that Bristol's planning policies enjoyed a large measure of cross-party and commercial support at least until the mid-sixties. What is represented today by some writers as a mass movement for change in planning matters was never extensive and in its very early days made up of a handful of far-sighted architects whose major concerns lay more in the field of design than overall planning.

The major decisions made in the forties which were effected and have therefore shaped the city centre area as we now know it were simple. There were just two. One was to build the Inner Circuit Road, which was mostly complete by the mid-sixties. Since then, only the M32 link to the M4 and the pedestrianisation of Broadmead, Deanery Road and Queens Square have been completed and the latter three were all aspirations of the Planning Committee when the author left it in 1968. The second decision was to move the main shopping centre from its traditional site in the Castle Street/Wine Street area down the hill in a northerly direction to Broadmead. It is possible to trace all the main subsequent decisions, at least until 1970, from these two early schemes. Those who seek to criticise the fifties and sixties planning of Bristol have much on their side, particularly in the part of the debate concerned with conservation, but whether these views, if applied at the time, would have given Bristol the mobility and commercial success which went with the fifties schemes is open to doubt.

In these years, the Planning Committee had a number of leading figures as Chairman, but none so well known to the public as Alderman Gervas Walker of the Citizen Party and Alderman Walter Jenkins of the Labour Party. The latter was Chairman in the mid-sixties and Alderman Walker discharged the office from 1967 to 1972. In later years, it has become a careless habit of local historians to argue that both men operated a bi-partisan policy in planning that amounted to a consensus. This is to do less than justice to each of them. The author served for several years under both men and can recall serious policy disagreements in a number of areas. Where they were unanimous was in a selfless commitment of service to the city and their decisions should always be researched and analysed against that background. This must also be said. Apart from the Bristol Architects Forum opposition to the Wine Street proposals in 1959/60, which was based on planning objections, the alternative proposals of the environment groups, in particular the Bristol Civic Society, consisted of conservation and preservation of old buildings, mostly Georgian, residential and all badly run-down. While the Walker years produced for the city a viable road pattern and an office-based commercial economy which still serves Bristol well today, the conservationists' alternative may well have produced a preserved, genteel and inactive suburbia. Be that as it may, the debate on these issues had, by the late sixties, produced an active conservation lobby in Bristol, articulate and alive to every move the Planning Committee made.

In the early months of 1969, the City Council moved to promote a Bill in Parliament which sought to close the City Docks to navigation. It also included a programme of works to dam the New Cut at Ashton and abandon the Feeder Canal which would have been filled in. In the early stages of the discussion, and long before the matter became public, the proposals were put before the Executive Committee of the Citizen Party which at that time had a large majority on the Council. In the plans that went down on the table that evening, the scheme to 'reclaim' parts of the harbour stood out from all the rest. The author, who was present, joined others in pointing out that they could not support this part of the scheme and it was sent back for modification, leaving the harbour as it was and is. After this there was never any prospect of the plan to fill the harbour succeeding as it would not have got a majority in council. City officials, however, went ahead and published the details.

Immediately, there was a public outcry of the sort so dear to the heart of the true Bristolian. The people worst hit were those firms still trading in the docks: the sand interests and Charles Hill & Sons, the shipbuilders at Albion Dockyard. They promptly entered objections to the Bill and were joined by a strong conservation lobby, prominent among which were the Civic Society, the Cabot Cruising Club and the Inland Waterways Association. The conservation groups were concerned with the road plans which proposed new bridges across the entrance of St. Augustine's Reach and from Cumberland

Road across the harbour to join Jacob's Wells Road. Both measures were highly controversial and the conservationists felt that the end of navigation rights would give the road builders a free hand.

Civic bills promoted by a council, if opposed, must go before a town meeting and, if not accepted, then to a town poll. An argumentative Town Meeting was held at the Colston Hall on December 15th 1969 which saw the Corporation face their critics in an atmosphere which often descended into outright uproar. The outcome was inevitable – the Bill was rejected. Most accounts end at this point, indicating that the whole thing had been a triumph for the conservation lobbies. However, there was a sequel, as the Council now had no option but to call a Town Poll and both sides took their case to the electorate. This was without precedent in a modern British city, although the practice is commonplace in the U.S.A. In the event the Council won a significant victory, votes for the Bill totalling 22,298 with 16,274 against.

Ashmead's tug *Thelmleigh*.

So the Bill went forward after all, and in Select Committee of the House of Lords, its many clauses benefited from that establishment's two great contributions to British democracy – restraint and common sense. In the end, the Bill became the Bristol Corporation Act 1971 when Royal Assent was granted on July 27th that year. The Act gave specific guarantees to the sand interests and to Charles Hill and Co., particularly to long serving employees of the latter, which were only equitable but little understood when later revealed.

41

In the end, as the Queen of Hearts remarked to Alice, everyone had won and everyone had to have prizes. The sand trade was protected, the shipyard was guaranteed compensation in the event of closure, the conservationists had 'won the fight for Bristol', in their view at any rate, and the Corporation had got its Bill.

The problems of the future use of the deserted quays and waterways was far from solved, however. The Port Authority rightly thought itself a commercial organisation. By the end of 1972, it was handling only 20,000 tonnes of cargo in the City Docks and was quite content to transfer all the assets to the Planning Committee. In due course, after a valiant struggle by Richard Hill to keep Albion Dockyard open, in which he received not a penny of the subsidies that went to other yards, Charles Hill's launched their last ship *Miranda Guinness* on July 9th 1976, and then closed their doors on an era that had seen the *Arethusa* and the *Favell*. Another era closed when the last of a series of Royal Naval Reserve drillships, the sloop H.M.S. *Flying Fox* was towed away for scrap. One of the ugliest warships ever built, she was named after the Derby winner of 1890 and served at Mardyke from 1923 to 1973. She left Bristol on Sunday March 18th 1973 and the RNVR Severn Division now operates from a 'stone frigate' in Winterstoke Road. The modern minesweeper H.M.S. *Carron* provides sea training based in Avonmouth old dock.

There has been, of course, a postscript which continues to this day. In the event, the Bristol Corporation Act 1971 gave Bristol powers which the new council created as a district authority in 1974 did not have the financial strength to implement. So the Act was abandoned on April 13th 1976 and the waterways are still operated to the plans of Jessop who designed them two hundred years ago. Development of the quayside has been piecemeal, but nonetheless attractive, and the quays have become home to many sailing ships like *Inca*, the ill-fated *Marques* that was knocked down in a squall in the Bermuda Triangle, the *Irene*, *Pascual Flores* and the Square Sail Fleet based at A Shed, headed by their good looking ship-rigged *Kaskelot*.

The story of the building of the Maritime Heritage Centre is told elsewhere in this narrative. The timber wharves at Baltic Wharf lay fallow for over a decade while the Council pursued plans to build local authority housing on the site. Then, in 1983, political control of the Council changed briefly for a year. The author sent for incoming Housing Chairman Marmaduke Alderson and told him to get on with a housing scheme immediately. 'Leave it to me,' he said. Alderson was as good as his word and the attractive development at Baltic Wharf is the result. Five years were to pass before the next major development in the docks area, the Lloyds Bank scheme which received planning permission in October 1988 and led to the spectacular demolition of the Tobacco Bonds. At the time of writing, development on the rest of Canon's Marsh seems as far away as ever.

Today, hundreds of pleasure craft crowd the quays where once the coastal ships came and went. A marina occupies the Albion Dockyard but the sand boats still come and go and there are regular visits from R.N. and NATO navy ships. *Balmoral* winters at Princes Wharf and the cross yards of the Square Sail vessels rise on the skyline. As long as they do so, something of the old spirit of Bristol will remain.

A pound for a paddle steamer

"The steamer service up and down the Channel between Bristol, Clevedon, Weston-super-Mare, Lynmouth and Ilfracombe, is made as far as possible a daily one; but owing to the tides it occasionally happens that these excursions are not run from Bristol for a day or so."

Messrs. P. & A. Campbells Bristol Channel Guide – 1923 edition.

Ever since the days of May, 1887, when the muddy waters of the Bristol Channel were first churned by the paddlewheels of a Campbell steamer, a favourite day out for Bristolians had been to 'go down 'Combe with Campbells'. The smart little steamers, with their black hulls, gold band and white upperworks all crowned with a spotless white funnel belching acrid black smoke, were very popular and each summer attracted good business.

Most popular of all was the fleet flagship, the *Britannia*, 459 grt, which was built in 1896 and served her owners for exactly sixty years! Daily during the summer season as the tide in the Avon allowed, the *Britannia* left Hotwells landing stage for Clevedon, Weston-super-Mare and Ilfracombe prompt at 9 a.m. Apart from the years of the Great War 1914–18, this service was uninterrupted for the first four decades of this century until all the Campbell services were suspended on September 2nd 1939 as Hitler's panzers tore into Poland.

Veterans who can recall *Britannia* excursions (and they get fewer with the passing of the years) always mention the excitement of catching the tram along St. George's Road to Hotwells, where *Britannia* would be waiting at the landing stage, having come out through the Cumberland Basin locks from her overnight berth in Underfall Yard. By 1939, the fare to Ilfracombe had risen to a stiff 8 shillings day return – quite a sum when the national average wage was something under £3 per week of 44 hours. As soon as one was on board, there were three choices. One could stay on deck for the sights as *Britannia* proceeded under Brunel's suspension bridge at a sedate speed down the Avon to the sea. Then there was always the attraction of the engine room, where the

45

great piston rods and valve gear were open for all to see as they rotated smoothly (in a high state of polish) to drive the ship through the water. Finally, if one could afford it, there was the chance to eat a slap-up breakfast at the cost of 1/6d in the spotlessly clean dining saloon, attended by equally spotless stewards. These paddle steamer saloons have become part of the legend of the paddle steamer, no doubt much of it due to the less than acceptable standards of food and cleanliness that one had to suffer in later years.

The other subject that veterans enjoy discussing is that of *Britannia*'s speed, particularly when compared with her near sister, the *Cambria* which was built a year earlier. Both ships had identical sets of engines but Lloyds Register always quoted *Cambria*'s speed as 20.5 knots, giving her sister an extra half knot! 21 knots is a goodly speed for a ship even today but it seems that if these steamers were lightly loaded and had their side scuttles fully open, then they could achieve speeds of this order. The author can remember, in the mid-sixties, the Campbell managing director Clifton Smith-Cox allowing *Bristol Queen*'s master, Captain Jack George, permission to overtake the Swedish liner *Gripsholm* which the paddler had been tendering in Walton Bay, off Clevedon. The big liner set off down channel at 18 knots or more, only for her crew to see *Bristol Queen* go tearing past, all scuttles open and ensign aloft at a good 20 knots! Delighted American tourists were heard to exclaim "Elmer, we're being overtaken by a side wheeler!"

When war broke out in 1939, Campbells had eleven paddlers in their fleet, with a big screw driven vessel of 2,000 tons on order for the 'no passport' cross channel excursion trade from south coast resorts. Bristol was not to see this new acquisition until June 1947. The entire fleet was pressed into service in the Royal Navy, only *Ravenswood* maintaining a Cardiff–Weston ferry for a few weeks in early 1940. First as minesweepers, then as anti-aircraft ships, the little paddlers were in the thick of the action from first to last, particularly at the Dunkirk beaches in 1940 and then in the return to France on the Normandy beaches in June 1944. When eventually victory was achieved and the ships began to trickle back to Bristol in 1945, no fewer than five had been lost – *Devonia*, *Brighton Queen* and *Brighton Belle* at Dunkirk, *Waverley* in the North Sea and *Glen Avon* off the Normandy beaches. Two others, *Cambria* and *Westward Ho*, were worn out and considered to be unworthy of refit.

Despite the war losses and the period of national austerity that followed, the Campbell board boldly determined to rebuild the fleet of paddle steamers and announced orders for the two largest ships of that type that the company had ever constructed. In the light of future events, it was a brave, even risky decision, but the initial results were the *Bristol Queen* and *Cardiff Queen*, two fine ships that lasted until the end of the sixties. *Bristol Queen* was built by Charles Hill at Albion Dockyard and they made a fine job. A good looking, powerful ship, she was the first in the Campbell fleet to have triple expansion engines by Rankin and Blackmore, who at the same time were producing an identical set for the new L.N.E.R. Clyde steamer *Waverley*, of which more later. Although Campbells wanted to place the contract for the second ship with Hills, that yard was so busy that early delivery could not be guaranteed and the order for *Cardiff Queen* went to the Fairfield Yard on the Clyde, which also built the engines. To the author, who got to know both ships well over the years, the *Cardiff Queen* never quite had the quality and style of the Bristol ship, which was usually chosen for the longer excursions and charters, while *Cardiff Queen* spent much of her time on the Cardiff–Weston ferry.

Bristol Queen was launched by the Lady Mayoress of Bristol, Mrs. John Owen on April 4th 1946. At the launch there was a curious repetition of history, when, as with the *Great Britain* over a century earlier, two attempts were necessary to smash a bottle on the ship's bow, although on this occasion the bottle contained 'Bristol Milk', the celebrated local blend of sherry.

Eight days later, on April 11th 1946, a much re-fitted *Ravenswood* opened the post-war services from Bristol with an excursion to Walton Bay and Clevedon that was timed to leave at 3.30 p.m. An hour before sailing time, the queue of intending passengers stretched half a mile back along Hotwell Road and *Ravenswood* sailed fully loaded, leaving hundreds disappointed on the quayside.

Bristol Queen was ready by September 1946 and she was joined by *Cardiff Queen* in the following year. The new screw ship, *Empress Queen*, was also available after her war service, though she proved to be an unprofitable liability. Denied her planned trade by Government currency restrictions on cross-channel trips to France, she spent four seasons blundering alongside south coast piers for which she was not designed, and it came as no surprise when she was laid up in St. Augustines Reach, Bristol at the Pierhead in 1952. For two years, she was a familiar sight to Bristolians as they caught their buses at the Centre, until she was eventually sold to Greek buyers and sailed under her own power to the Piraeus in March 1955.

The six paddle steamers now operated services that were limited versions of pre-war runs. In 1947, the *Glen Gower* returned to Brighton, while the other operated in the Bristol Channel. Traffic was reasonable in the late forties, with petrol still rationed, and this despite the shortage of piers on the Channel as a result of the repair work which was required following military use. Minehead pier had disappeared altogether. The rot set in during the early fifties, as families which before the war would have thought car ownership beyond their means, now began to acquire motor transport in their millions. Passenger figures fell and in 1954 a loss of £54,000 was reported. 1955 was better, with more passengers carried to Ilfracombe than in any year since 1924.

It was the 1956 season that marked a turning point in the history of Bristol and ended the close connection of the firm with the city that it had held since 1888. The weather that season was bad and a meeting of shareholders in Bristol on July 26th were told that the loss was likely to be £74,000, bringing the total liabilities to over £250,000. To reduce the deficit, the company's headquarters were moved to Cardiff as the Welsh port now provided the bulk of passengers, and the lease of Underfall Yard from the P.B.A. was discontinued. In future, the ships were registered in Cardiff, carried the Red Dragon flag at the jackstaff and operated from offices in Lower Bute Street, just on the edge of Tiger Bay. To Bristolians, it was just as if part of their city had been torn away. Although the Port Authority tried to assist the company by giving it very preferential rates for the use of Hotwells Landing Stage, sailings from Bristol were to be sparse in the years that followed.

The year 1957 saw Campbell's withdrawal from services from both Newport and Brighton, three ships were laid up in 1958 and by late 1959 the business was in receivership. However, the entire assets and liabilities were taken over by George Nott Industries Ltd., among whose many interests was the Townsend-Thoresen ferry group. With this kind of backing, the early sixties saw a new lease of life and the company bought its first motorship, the *St. Trillo*, in 1963 and added a second, the *Westward Ho*, in 1965. The arrival of the motor vessels and the reduced passenger traffic sealed the fate of the paddle steamers. Lovely as these ships were, their high fuel consumption and manning requirements made them thoroughly uneconomic. *Cardiff Queen* was withdrawn in 1966 and *Bristol Queen* a year later, following damage suffered in collision with a submerged object off Barry. Thus the 1968 season was started with an all-motor vessel fleet, enhanced by a charter of the Scilly Isles reserve ship *Queen of the Isles*. This latter was a 515 ton motor ship built in Bristol in 1964 by Charles Hill and fitted out to that yard's usual high standards. The Scilly Isles trade never really justified the building of a second ship for the service and the *Queen* spent much of her time on charter until she was sold to the Tongan Government in 1970 for inter-island services.

The summer of 1969 saw the first arrival on the Bristol Channel of the motor ship *Balmoral*, an ex-Isle-of-Wight ferry, surprising channel veterans with her speed and excellent handling qualities. "The best ship Campbells ever had!" was the opinion of the late Captain Jack Wide, who commanded her for several

Paddlesteamer *Glen Usk* at Ilfracombe.

seasons and ought to have known. *Balmoral*'s success was overshadowed by the continuing bad state of repair of the channel piers. Cardiff, Barry and Weston were all in poor condition and the problem was highlighted on October 17th 1970 when two spans of Clevedon Pier fell into the Channel while under strength tests. These years therefore saw the nadir of the excursion services and after the withdrawal of *St. Trillo* and *Westward Ho*, by 1971 *Balmoral* was the only, and as it turned out the last, ship in the Campbell fleet. In 1971, Campbells announced that most of their activities would take place in the lower channel between Swansea, Mumbles, Ilfracombe and Lundy, with only occasional calls at Bristol, Weston and Penarth. For the following nine seasons *Balmoral* kept the Campbell burgee flying on the Channel, thanks largely to the single-minded determination of Clifton Smith-Cox to keep the company afloat. A bad summer in 1979, however, coinciding with the withdrawal of Townsend support, gave the future a very uncertain look. Then a deal with the Landmark Trust, managers of Lundy, was announced for the 1980 season.

The Landmark Trust had been running Lundy since 1969 when the island was bought by the National Trust, solely due to the generosity of Jack Hayward, the Bahamas-based property developer who presented the island to the nation for the asking price of £150,000, as a token of his gratitude to his native Great Britain. Mr. Hayward was already committed to save the s.s. *Great Britain*. Communications with the Devon mainland have always proved a serious problem for successive owners of Lundy and the agreement with Campbells for *Balmoral* to tender the island in 1980 was the latest scheme of many over the years. The arrangement did not prove a happy one and was terminated after one season, after which Campbells ceased trading, Weston Pier was sold and the landing stage closed, and *Balmoral* laid up at Bristol. With her was the *Devonia*, another ex-Scilly Isles ferry which Campbells had bought in 1977 for oil rig support work for the Townsend Group. The two ships were a familiar sight at Prince's Wharf in the City Docks for months, even being cast adrift by vandals one dark night and gently drifting around the harbour. Then *Devonia* was sold to Torquay owners for Jersey services and *Balmoral* went north to Dundee to become a floating restaurant. The P.B.A. closed the landing stage at Hotwells and allowed it to rot. Part was later demolished, and everyone thought that that was that. Pleasure steamer services on the Bristol Channel had ended at last. That the excursions had continued for so long was due largely to the enthusiasm of Clifton Smith-Cox. He had joined the Campbell board in 1952 and become sole Managing Director in 1955. For over a quarter of a century he steered the company and gave Bristol and the west country excursion services long after such trips had disappeared from other coastal areas. Well past normal retirement age, Clifton now went on to build up the highly successful Mount Charlotte hotel chain. His death in 1990 saddened several generations of channel travellers who recalled his genial presence on the steamers, lending a hand with any job that needed doing.

Amazingly, there was to be a sequel and it came about because of the determination of a handful of devoted men and women. Back in 1959, when it looked as if paddle steamers were about to disappear not only from the Bristol Channel but from the entire British coasts, Professor Alan Robinson, then of the University of Wales, founded the Paddle Steamer Preservation Society with the ultimate objective of acquiring and running its own ship. There was no great rush of membership and the shipping industry looked on with scarcely concealed amusement. "Why not stick to steam locomotives?" enquired one Bristol shipowner of the author as he was trying to save the *Bristol Queen* in 1967. Nevertheless, from very small beginnings the group was soon publishing a quarterly magazine, *Paddle Wheels*, which it used for historical articles on the one hand and the promotion of paddle steamer travel on the other. Soon, branches of the Society grew up in those parts of the United Kingdom where paddle steamers were well remembered – the south coast, the Bristol Channel, the Clyde and the Thames. Early attempts to save particular steamers came to naught but the Society soldiered on and bided its time.

The breakthrough came in 1974 when Caledonian Macbrayne, the Scots islands ferry operators offered their last working sea-going paddler *Waverley* to the Scottish branch of the Society for £1! One has to say 'sea-going' as the p.s. *Maid of the Loch* was still afloat on Loch Lomond. *Waverley* dated from the same years as the Campbell *Queens* and running her was an expensive business which needed the experience and judgement of professionals. A company, Waverley Steam Navigation, was formed by the backers of the project among whom Douglas MacGowan and Terry Sylvester were prominent. The ship was vested in a trust and, most important of all, the services of a master mariner, in all senses of the word, were obtained in Captain David Neill, whose contribution to the *Waverley* project ensured its success. *Waverley* began her new career in May 1975 and, through a whole list of triumphs and, it must be said, misfortunes, she continues in service to this day, still largely under David Neill's command.

It was soon apparent that the Clyde could not produce enough traffic to sustain *Waverley* in service and the decision was taken to run her in other parts of the country. So it was that David Neill brought a paddle steamer back to the Bristol Channel at the end of May 1979. By this time, the heritage movement in Britain was getting into its stride, preservation schemes were blossoming to conserve just about every mechanical contrivance that humanity had devised, from sewing machines to jet airliners. *Waverley* was given a rapturous welcome everywhere she called and she has returned every year since.

When it became apparent that *Waverley* was going to fulfil the expectations of her backers, it was logical to propose the acquisition of a second ship to back her up. In 1981, a group of business people connected with the project, but acting independently, bought the Isle-of-Wight ferry *Shanklin*, refitted her on the Clyde and brought her to Bristol for excursion work on May 1st 1981 under the new name *Prince Ivanhoe*. She attracted good crowds but the high promise of the venture ended in disaster when she was holed on rocks off the Gower Coast on August 3rd of the same year, while operating on a very low tide. Captain Neill was in command at the time and he took the immediate decision to beach the ship in Port Eynon Bay. This timely action saved the lives of all on board but *Prince Ivanhoe* was a total loss, being broken up on the spot.

Much happier was the return of *Balmoral* to Bristol from exile in Dundee in 1986. When the *Waverley* project looked for another back-up ship, it was thought that the elderly engines of *Balmoral* would no longer be in working condition. A visit to Dundee by project engineers found the ship in remarkable condition for such an old vessel built in 1948, and, even better, she was for sale. So, after a rebuild aft to improve her passenger accommodation, and sporting a new paint job of 'cruising white', *Balmoral* arrived back in the Avon on April 12th 1986 to the cheers of a large crowd at Cumberland Basin. Registered in Bristol, the ship has now been adopted by many Bristol people and society members who work aboard during winter refits which are carried out in Bristol. Practical support from the Bristol City Council in the shape of free berthing facilities has helped to ensure *Balmoral*'s continued running.

Finally, as if to crown all these efforts with a major success, Clevedon Pier re-opened to steamer traffic on Saturday, May 27th 1989, after years of valiant fund raising by its supporters. The story of the pier restoration has been told elsewhere. It was a long and often heart breaking struggle against ever rising costs and local authority indifference. The pier supporters triumphed in the end and now the pier provides a considerable boost to *Waverley* and *Balmoral*.

As the crowds hurry to catch the departing ships, almost always on the quayside is to be seen the busy, likeable figure of Commander Tom Foden, R.N. Retd., who has been agent on the Bristol Channel for both ships. His contribution as the public face of the ships has been of crucial importance. Today *Waverley* and *Balmoral* sail to many places which have not received call for years, if ever. The island of Steepholm, off Weston in mid-channel and full of interest, is a regular call and such places as far distant as Sharpness and Truro have been visited. Anywhere which has a secure quay wall, three bollards and enough water is certain to catch the attention of the route planners. Both ships regularly operate all around the British mainland and are frequent visitors to Ireland. In 1992, they have been working in partnership with the Landmark Trust's m.v. *Oldenberg* which has travelled as far north as Gloucester, along the Sharpness canal. For some years in the late eighties, *Waverley* and *Balmoral* were banned from Lundy following a disagreement between the two organisations but that is now happily in the past.

Both Campbells and Waverley Steam Navigation can take pride in their history and their record of service to thousands of excursionists, past and present. Their ships have appeared consistently in coastal waters of the West country for over a century. Long after the end of each season, when the paddles of *Waverley* have ceased to stir the muddy waters of the Avon, Bristol people recall those summer mornings when they take a bus to Hotwells or Clevedon. There the *Waverley* is waiting to cast off for another trip 'down Combe'. Memories of those golden days and lovely ships will persist when far more important matters are long forgotten.

The much loved *Waverley* on the Avon.

Any old iron?

"Cunard Line has enough old iron already."

*The Late Lord Mancroft, then Deputy
Chairman of Cunard, when asked to
contribute to the restoration of
the s.s.* Great Britain *in 1970.*

At the Redcliffe end of Queen Square, almost next to the Hole-in-the-Wall, stands a derelict Georgian building which for many years housed the Bristol Sailors' Home. Maintained as a charity by Bristol shipowners, the home offered a refuge to sailors in the port who were down on their luck. With the passing of the commercial trade from the city docks, the home became redundant and has long since closed. In its heyday the home was for many years the headquarters of the Bristol Shiplovers Society which held a monthly meeting there every winter season.

The society was founded in 1930 to offer membership to anyone in the city who loved ships and the sea and it has flourished ever since. Inevitably it attracted a large number of retired sailors into its ranks and a visit to one of its meetings usually turned into a fascinating discussion about long lost ships and distant voyages. On the rare occasion that the discussion flagged, it was always renewed by the society's long serving secretary George Paton who had served in Cunard as a deck officer and never lacked for a good yarn. His death in 1991 saddened Bristol's maritime community and removed an unforgettable character from the scene.

If anyone is to be credited with starting maritime conservation in Bristol, it must be the Bristol Shiplovers Society. Early in their history, the members started a collection of maritime artefacts which has grown steadily over the years. Some have been handed over to the City Museum, among which is a ship's figurehead restored by members of the society and the bell of the aircraft carrier H.M.S. *Argus* complete with belfry. The latter was presented in memory of the late Canon Percival Gay of St. George's Church, Great George Street who served as chaplain on *Argus* for most of the war and was honorary chaplain to the Shiplovers.

The first attempt at preserving a complete ship was in 1937 when the society made a forlorn attempt to save the barque *Favell* from the shipbreakers. The *Favell* is important in Bristol's maritime history as the last sailing ship to be built in the city and the Shiplovers had already adopted her as the vessel that appeared on their membership badge. She was built by Charles Hill at Albion Dockyard in 1895 as a speculative venture and operated by them for two years until the firm decided the time had come to get out of sailing ships. *Favell* was sold to Finnish owners and eventually ended up in the hands of the famous Captain Gustav Eriksen of Mariennam in the Aaland Islands who ran her in the Australian grain trade. When finally he sent *Favell* for scrap in 1937, after a lay-up from 1934, the Shiplovers Society appealed to the Port Authority and some of Bristol's shipowners to bring the ship back to Bristol as a museum piece. Today there would be at least a dozen bids from around the world for such an attractive ship, such is the interest in commercial theme parks, but in 1937 the idea was considered to border on the insane by Bristol's maritime community. The only useful ship was the one at sea, fully laden and making money. It was a view that was to persist and one that came within a whisker of keeping the s.s. *Great Britain* out of Bristol. So the *Favell* went for scrap and all that remains of her is a small bell in the possession of the Shiplovers which is regularly used to strike 'eight bells' at the conclusions of society meetings.

After the war, apart from the R.N.V.R. drill ships *Flying Fox* and *Locust*, the only example of a preserved vessel to be discovered by a visitor to the City Docks was the *John Sebastian*, an elderly lightship that had served on the English and Welsh Grounds station, the spot where the deep water channel into Avonmouth swings towards the southern bank of the Severn estuary. Now she was in retirement as the floating clubhouse of the Cabot Cruising Club and was the only retired ship on the Floating Harbour when, in 1967, there occurred another opportunity to preserve a famous Bristol ship. This time it was the powerful Campbell paddler *Bristol Queen*, the last of an historic line of steamers using that form of propulsion, and the only Campbell ship built in Bristol. On August 28th 1967, *Bristol Queen* had hit a submerged object, probably a log, off Barry and lost a paddle blade and arm from the starboard wheel. Three days later she was taken out of service and laid up at Cardiff. In September of the same year, it was announced that she was for sale at an asking price of £10,000.

Bristol City Museum were anxious to acquire the ship as a floating maritime museum and, for once the City Council was prepared to consider the idea. At the time the author had been a councillor for nine years and was beginning to know his way around. He got authority from the then leader, Gervas Walker, to do a preliminary inspection of the ship with the museum director Alan

Wharhurst. By then, the *Bristol Queen* had been hit by a passing tramp steamer and damaged again but not seriously. The scheme looked feasible but then the commercial factor intervened. The managing director of Campbells, Clifton Smith-Cox, was also the Chairman of the Bristol Grand Hotel Company and a condition of the sale of the ship was that no catering activity was allowed on board to compete with the company's hotels. Such a condition made it almost impossible to run an even modest economic scheme and so *Bristol Queen* went for scrap in Belgium. Twenty three years later, her ship's wheel came up for auction in Plymouth and is now in Bristol, in the possession of the author.

Three years later, in mid-1970, the preservation situation in the port was stood on its head by the arrival back in Bristol of the s.s. *Great Britain*, Brunel's iron steamship, built in the city between 1840 and 1845. One of the most historic ships of all time, the *Great Britain* had been in the Falkland Islands since 1886 after being written off as incapable of repair following storm damage. Until 1937 she performed a useful function as a floating wool store, a fairly vital function to a community where the only useful domesticated animal is the sheep. In 1937 the ship became redundant and was towed from Port Stanley to nearby Sparrow Cove where she was abandoned to the elements, by the simple process of knocking several holes in her bottom. Incredibly, the *Great Britain* survived this process. In the latter stages of her career, her sides had been cladded in teak before she was commissioned as a nitrate carrier in the Chilean trade. This curious act was alleged to be for protection against damage to the ship's iron hull from nitrate barges that came alongside to discharge cargo. Whatever the reason, the wood tended to protect the hull from corrosion and iron in any case is far more rust resistant than steel. The pure clear air of the South Atlantic is probably the cleanest on earth. Indeed, the corrosion rate of the iron in the old hull increased dramatically when, in Bristol, it was exposed to the air pollution created by industry in Avonmouth and South Wales.

The story of the return of the *Great Britain* to the dock in Bristol has been related in detail by Richard Goold-Adams in his book *The Return of the Great Britain* (Weidenfeld and Nicholson, 1976) and of its repair, in Commander Joe Blake's *Restoring the Great Britain* (Redcliffe Press, 1989). The relationship between the project organisers and the City Council was often less than happy and it may be appropriate to place on record the facts about how the ship was allowed to enter the port. There were two main factors at work in the stance taken by some senior members of the council at that time, the summer of 1969. Following Dr. Ewan Corlett's letter to *The Times* of November 7th 1967, a committee under the chairmanship of Richard Goold-Adams had started

The R.N.V.R. drill ship *Flying Fox* on the Hotwells waterfront.

fundraising to salvage the ship and return her to the U.K. This same summer, the committee obtained the welcome financial support of Jack Hayward, a great patriot who provided funds to get the ship afloat and back to Bristol. With the scheme now looking a real possibility rather than fantasy, the powers-that-be in Bristol had to declare their attitude to the project. The first reaction was the usual one. Any ship not earning money had no place but the scrapyard. By 1970 this was not any longer a valid argument to many people but the second objection had more substance. After the years of neglect, the condition of the *Great Britain*'s hull was less than sound and the Port Authority now raised the possibility of her sinking during the very last stage of her 8,000 mile journey – in the close confines of the River Avon in the five miles between Bristol and the sea. Although the deep sea trade had left the City Docks by that time, and the Council was in the throes of an acrimonious debate about closure of navigation rights, the possibility of an accident had to be taken seriously.

A decision on whether to admit the *Great Britain* to Bristol was needed before anything else could happen and here politics took a hand. In 1969, the City Council was controlled by the Citizen Party, a curious Bristol anachronism which in reality meant the Conservative Party. On the evening of Friday, July 4th 1969, the party group meeting held a long internal debate on whether to admit the ship or not. Eventually a motion to admit, moved by the present author, was carried by 17 votes to 15. This motion was therefore accepted as group and council policy. After this decision, the city's welcome to the ship was assured.

Anyone who was present at the towing of *Great Britain* up the River Avon is unlikely ever to forget the occasion. Thousands of people lined the river banks as the tugs gently eased the ageing old lady towards her final retirement home. The author was fortunate to be on board the P.B.A. launch, with the Lord Mayor, Alderman Geoffrey Palmer. All those who had made this one of the great days in Bristol's long maritime history earned the gratitude of Bristol and the city took the *Great Britain* to its heart. There would be many more arguments, for example about insurance, before the ship finally settled onto the blocks of the Great Western Dry Dock where she had been built in the 1840s. The date of the drydocking was July 19th 1970 and H.R.H. Prince Philip was on board, giving the seal of Royal approval. After that, fund raising proceeded, the ship was opened to the public and the long task of restoration was put in hand.

In the two decades since 1970, the appearance of the ship has changed until now she looks much as she did in 1845. Dr. Basil Greenhill, the distinguished maritime historian and conservationist succeeded Richard Goold-Adams in the chair of the project and H.R.H. Prince Andrew, Duke of York has become Patron. Jack Hayward has once again been a principal benefactor as has Mr. John Paul Getty. A remarkable part of the restoration has been that of the dining room which opened for public functions in 1992, in which year Dr. Greenhill was succeeded by Sir Richard Gaskell, a past President of the Law Society. In this year also, the University of Bristol honoured Richard Goold-Adams for his achievement with the honorary degree of Master of Arts. At the degree ceremony, the Public Orator was Richard Hill, the Bristol shipowner and shipbuilder who did so much to ease the difficulties that arose in the ship's recovery and restoration. Today, the s.s. *Great Britain* ranks alongside H.M.S. *Victory*, H.M.S. *Warrior*, *Cutty Sark* and U.S.S. *Constitution* as one of the world's great ship restoration projects.

The return of the hull of the s.s. *Great Britain*.

In retrospect, the return of the *Great Britain* marked the turning point in the history of Bristol's City Docks: the point at which commercial shipping ceased as the main activity and leisure and conservation took over. At first the going was slow. Other priorities made the finding of funds for the City Docks difficult, as when in 1971, the seemingly everlasting prefab bungalows, built after the war as a temporary solution to the housing crisis, began to show serious structural defects. The Chairman of the Housing Committee, Derek

St. Augustine's Reach.

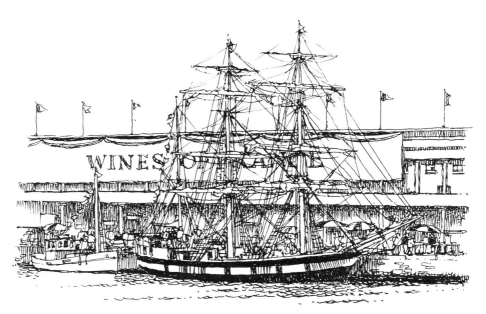

A maritime visitor to the Wine Fair.

Topham, showed characteristic courage in undertaking to replace 3,000 prefabs by 1976, but it all took money. In May of the same year, Bristolians got a rare glimpse of the underground River Frome when the Rupert Street culvert was opened for strengthening.

1973 saw the loss of a ship that had been part of the scene at St. Georges' Road, Hotwells, since 1923. The R.N.V.R. drillship H.M.S. *Flying Fox* was an anti-submarine sloop, built in the First World War and named after the Derby winner of 1890 as a member of the 'Racehorse' Class. This class was possibly one of the ugliest groups of warship ever to come from the drawing board of a naval architect. Yet generations of Bristol naval volunteers and reservists loved her and she served them well for half a century until 1973. She was then considered too small for modern requirements and the Severn Division of the R.N.V.R. moved ashore to a 'stone frigate', also called H.M.S. *Flying Fox*, located in buildings in Winterstoke Road, Bedminster. The old ship was towed away for scrap on Sunday, March 13th 1973 and a little bit of Bristol's history passed with her.

It was not until 1978 that maritime conservation took another step forward in the shape of the Bristol Industrial Museum. By this time, the initial shock of Local Government reorganisation had subsided somewhat and new personalities had began to emerge on the City Council. Among these was John McLaren, a younger Labour member who was Chairman of the new Land and Administration Committee. McLaren's committee had to decide the future of the redundant properties in the dock area. Led by McLaren, the Committee resolved to convert the transit sheds L and M at Wapping Wharf to museum use and the Bristol Industrial Museum opened in 1978. The shed used was a relatively new building, put up in 1952 to replace sheds destroyed by the Luftwaffe in 1941. The museum concentrates on local industry and transport and there is a very strong nautical section which contains a history of the City Docks. Also in the museum is a section on aeronautics which contains Bristol's only memento of the great Concorde supersonic airliner, the British examples of which were

The Royal Barge at Bristol Docks for the opening of the Maritime Heritage Centre, July 26th, 1985.

built in Bristol. When the nose mock up section, used during development, became redundant, the City Council was offered the relic at a knock down price which even they could not refuse. However, they expected BAC to deliver and install the mock up in the museum. At the time (1980) the author was a senior production manager at Filton and so got the job to price and organise – because, in the words of Filton's then Chief Executive Jack Jefferies "you're a b----y councillor!"

By the early eighties, the Hilhouse collection, a wonderful collection of ship models, naval architect's plans, marine paintings and a large number of other relics of the Charles Hill shipyard, came on to the market. This coincided with the first proposals for a Maritime Heritage Centre for the city. The National Maritime Museum at Greenwich bought the Hilhouse collection with a generous grant in aid from the National Heritage Fund. It retained the merchant ship designs for its research section and allotted the remainder of the collection to Bristol. This was on the understanding that Bristol provided a building for the collection.

1983 was election year in Bristol. Somewhat to everyone's surprise, the Conservatives became the largest group on the City Council and the author found himself the Leader of the new administration. As Bristol holds yearly elections for a third of the Council, it was obvious that power was unlikely to last very long and one had to move fast. On sending for the plans of the Maritime Heritage Centre, the author was astonished to find that the outgoing Labour group had no intention of going ahead unless the project could be built as a youth opportunities scheme! The new administration decided to proceed with the support of Robin Howell's Liberal Group and design work started. The English Tourist Board, the Area Museum Council and Harveys of Bristol Ltd, all provided grant aid and the Director of British Rail's Western Region, Bill Bradshaw, gave invaluable help in the negotiations to obtain railway land on the quayside alongside the s.s. *Great Britain*.

All this took the best part of a year to set up but in March 1984 the contract was let to Ferson Ltd, and the works inaugurated by the author on April 30th 1984. Three days later the Conservatives lost office in the local elections! It had been a close shave. The Council was still hung, but with Labour now the largest party. The car park for the Heritage Centre and the *Great Britain* project was a separate contract. Again with the help of the valiant Robin Howell, a majority was obtained to let the car park contract and so the Maritime Heritage Centre was completed. It was opened to the public by Her Majesty Queen Elizabeth II, accompanied by His Royal Highness the Duke of Edinburgh, on Friday July 26th 1985, in the Lord Mayoralty of Councillor Jack Bosdet.

Just off the waterfront: Wine Street today.

IX

The *Golden Hind* moored at the Arnolfini.
X

Redcliffe Backs.

XI

In the heart of the maritime city: St. Nicholas Street.

XII

The *Balmoral* passing the *Great Britain*.
XIII

The *Pride of Baltimore* with Clifton Wood in the
background.
XIV

A brigantine moored at Square Sail.
XV

Overlooking St. Augustine's Reach: the restored
Swallow Royal Hotel and Bristol Cathedral.

XVI

Nowadays, in the early nineties, there is a fleet of preserved vessels in the City Docks. Of considerable variety, they range from the twin screw motor vessel *Lochiel*, built by William Denny at Dumbarton in 1939 for Macbrayne's Western Isles Mail service and now a pub to the two masted topsail schooner *Pascuel Flores*, Spanish built in 1918, which arrived in the city in 1978. Now owned by the Nova Trust, the schooner is undergoing a very long term refit. Other familiar vessels are the trading ketch *Irene*, built in Bridgwater in 1907, the fleet of Squaresail based at the old New York shed and including the impressive square rigger *Kaskelot*, and the fleet watering vessel *Freshspring*, often placed in steam by its owner, Oswald Burgess. Among a growing number of vessels moored for commercial use are the converted barge Glass Boat at Bristol Bridge, the Lightship at Welsh Back, the coaster *Thekla* at The Grove and artist Vincent Neave's floating gallery, the dumbbarge *Glevum*, built by Charles Hill in 1955.

Around these larger vessels circulate the mass of small boats that now populate the old Floating Harbour. It is a colourful and ever-changing scene, presided over by the five masts and black funnel of the s.s. *Great Britain*. Every so often other conservation projects are proposed. One recent idea was the proposal to bring the ferry *Princess Marguerite* 8,000 miles from Vancouver to be a floating hotel in Bristol's Cumberland Basin. This one flopped when the Canadians decided to hang on to their ship, but there is no doubt that others will crop up as the years go on.

The *Main* visiting Bristol.

Along the river bank

"There is nothing, absolutely nothing so worth doing as messing about in boats."

The Water Rat in Kenneth Graham's The Wind in the Willows.

Like many other cities, Bristol's history has been created in large measure by the rivers that flow through and around it. The city itself sprang up around the place where the first practical crossing of the Avon was built and given the name in Anglo-Saxon Brycgstow – the place of the bridge – which over the years became Bristol. These 'places of the bridge' crop up all over England. Bridstow on the Wye near Ross is such another but it has remained a village. Bristol grew into an important city because of its location on waterways which its merchants could use as a highway to the open sea and the riches of the New World, its soldiers use as a means of defence and its population employ as an industrial resource and a water supply.

The Bristol Avon, to give it the full geographic title, rises on the edge of the Wiltshire Downs and flows down through Bradford, Bath and Bristol to the sea at Avonmouth. There are several Avons in the country because the word derives from the Celtic 'afon' which means simply river. Here at Avonmouth the river merges with the muddy saltwater of the Severn estuary and becomes a highway down channel past the islands of Steepholm and Flatholm, the resorts of Weston, Minehead and Ilfracombe, until it reaches Lundy and the Atlantic Ocean. To stand on the South Pier of the Royal Edward Entrance at Avonmouth opens up to the eye one of the most exciting vistas in the United Kingdom. To the north, the Severn Road Bridge spans the river with 3,240 feet of decking between its main piers. Opened by Queen Elizabeth II in 1966, it is among the world's top dozen suspension bridges. Immediately ahead, in mid-channel, the small pimple of rock is Denny Island and beyond rise the green hills of Gwent. In this summer of '92 there are also the first exploration rigs seeking bedrock for the foundations of the bridges of the second Severn Crossing, considered necessary to supplement the overloaded first crossing five miles to the north east. The graceful suspension bridge engineered by

The Severn Bridge.

Freeman Fox and Partners and the consortium headed by Taylor Woodrow is, together with the M4 and M5 motorways and the Avonmouth road bridge, the Bristol region's largest civil engineering work to be constructed in the years since the Second World War. The bridge itself has had a chequered history and required much repair and modification. The latest strengthening programme was due for completion in late 1992 and from then onwards a trouble-free period of operation is expected.

The largest civil engineering work in the Avonmouth area is invisible from where we stand on the South Pier but it jumps into the headlines occasionally. The Severn Tunnel, at 4.35 miles long, is still the longest direct railway tunnel in Great Britain and although it passed its centenary in 1986 it is still a remarkable engineering work. It handles the HST 125 diesel express trains of the modern railway with the same ease with which it handled the great *Kings* and *Castles* of the days of steam. An accident in December, 1991, when a diesel motorised unit ran into the back of an HST, put the tunnel on to the front pages as 400 passengers had to be rescued.

North of the Severn Road Bridge there have been two major changes to the scene. The old Severn Railway Bridge which crossed from Sharpness to Lydney has disappeared. Opened in 1879 to carry coal from the Forest of Dean across

The Sharpness-Gloucester Canal at Frampton-on-Severn.

to the Midland main line and to the Gloucester ship canal, it had twenty-one classic spans. One of these was brought down into the river by an oil barge which rammed it in darkness while off course on passage to Gloucester. The bridge was already redundant and the remaining spans were removed piecemeal for scrap. But as old industries and structures disappear, so others rise in their place. Nothing demonstrates this more clearly than the closure of the coal industry in the Forest of Dean on the west bank of the Severn, only for it to be replaced on the east bank by the great piles of two nuclear power stations at Berkeley and Oldbury which went up in the sixties. Such is 'progress' that already Berkeley Power Station has been closed down and no longer supplies power to the National Grid, but causes considerable anxiety about its continuing radioactivity.

To the south the wharves of the new Royal Portbury Dock and its attendant warehouses are clearly seen across the mouth of the Avon and the remains of the power station at Portishead (minus two of its four chimneys) stands out against the sky. It still towers above the dock that opened in 1879, was bought by Bristol City Council in September 1882 and closed in 1989. Beyond

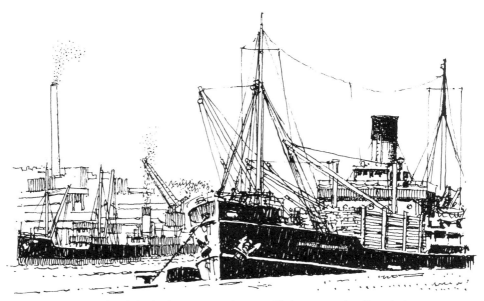

Portishead dock about 1950: *Agnette Christensen* unloading timber.

Clevedon.

Portishead, the river runs home to the sea, while alongside us the journey up river to Bristol begins.

The best way to see the Bristol Avon and to understand its impact on the city's history is to travel afloat as far as possible. Today, if one has the time and inclination it is possible to get as far as Bath by services available to the public at certain times. After that, the Kennet and Avon Canal is open all the way to Reading. The lower Avon below Bristol is no place for the amateur boatman, and the best way to make the passage is on the deck of an excursion steamer like *Waverley* or *Balmoral* or on one of *Tower Belle*'s or *Avon Venturer II*'s regular trips. At no time on a passage of the Avon is one unaware of the tide. It leaves its marks on the mudbanks on both sides, being a part of some of the most active water on Earth.

Twice every day, the tidal flow of the Bristol Channel gathers its strength in the waters around Lundy and charges irresistibly upstream to the north-east. In doing so it produces spring tides at Avonmouth, for example, of forty two feet, and the restless waters carry vast quantities of sediment. Approximately two million tons of mud are carried past Severn Beach on an ebb tide. By the time the gathering tides reach Avonmouth and meet the converging banks of the Severn, the tidal range can be anything up to fifty feet. That is fifty feet of vertical fall from high water to low. As all Bristol schoolchildren are taught, there is only one other place in the world that produces a higher tidal range. This is the Bay of Fundy, between the provinces of Nova Scotia and New Brunswick in Canada, where the Petitcodiac River produces a similar effect.

This Bristol Channel tide is not to be trifled with. In the course of a few hours, the raging torrent of the river is transformed into idle mudflats where oystercatchers scavenge or into pleasant-looking sandbanks on which the ignorant tread at their peril. Post-war accidents have been few but the river always takes its revenge on interference with its regime, or the ignoring of well tried local rules. As an example, in 1983, the replica galleon *Golden Hind* paid a visit to the City Docks, where she was the subject of great interest to Bristolians. As the vessel was registered as a yacht, her master was not required to take a pilot although, as he had to make two passages of the Avon, the advice of the river pilots might well have been an advantage, as the pilots were quick to point out before the vessel's arrival. Sure enough, as the *Golden Hind* left the river mouth at the end of her visit, on October 30th 1985, a stretch of fair water tempted whoever was at the wheel and he steered to port, going firmly aground on the south bank of the Avon. It was fortunate that, as the tide receded, the ship did not topple over, and she floated off on the next tide. *Golden Hind* actually grounded 56 minutes after high water, having left the

City Docks far too late to make the passage safely.

Another example of the capricious nature of the river tides was experienced by the Port Authority in 1988/89. The Docks Committee authorised occasional tipping of rubble at certain points at the mouth of the river, and also at Holesmouth, the long abandoned Second World War temporary oil wharf. The river made short work of the rubble, sweeping much of it away, but also setting up subsidiary sand and mud banks which had not been seen before. The practice of tipping ceased soon afterwards. Sometimes also, the river can be quite hostile to the wildlife that lives on and within it. The occasional seal will appear, finding the tide too strong for it to return to the open sea. On an October tide in 1972, a 15 foot whale was washed ashore below Severn Beach.

Incidents brought about by weather and tide continue to occur. There was a full scale emergency on May 9th 1992 when a dinghy race off Portishead was overwhelmed by sudden gale force squalls and 31 people had to be lifted from the water. Owing to economies in the eighties, there is only one coastguard station on the Channel, at Swansea. This adds time to rescue efforts in the upper river estuary. Swansea usually scramble the helicopters of No. 22 Squadron, R.A.F., which fly out of Chivenor in North Devon. Many people engaged in maritime affairs on the Bristol Channel find this reduction in rescue cover a matter for continuing concern.

Soon after it leaves Avonmouth and the port installations, the Avon passes under the M5 motorway bridge, which was opened to traffic in May 1974, after a three year construction period. A classic example of the box girder structure so beloved of contemporary civil engineers, the bridge carries the motorway across the Avon in an elegant loop which allows 90 feet of clearance for vessels on a high spring tide, a requirement of the Port Authority, which was still operating the City Docks when the bridge specification was drawn up. On a summer weekend it is now the busiest bridge in England, carrying well over half the holiday trade that passes into and out of the West country.

On the port side of the river, or the northern bank, just upstream from the bridge there was built in 1968/69 a new concrete quay structure to accommodate the city's new sludge disposal vessel *Glen Avon*, then under construction at the Ailsa Shipbuilding Company's yard at Troon in Ayrshire. In the sixties the City Engineer, James Bennett, undertook a large programme of major sewage disposal works with the aim of eventually removing all sewage disposal from the city's rivers and waterways, a process that started as far back as Brunel and was not to be completed until the eighties. In a warm summer, the odour from the river could become quite oppressive and the news of the scheme was greeted with relief by Bristolians. A large sewage treatment plant was built at the Avonmouth end of Kingsweston Lane and treated sludge pumped through pipes to the quay on the Avon. Here it is loaded onto *Glen Avon*, which carries it for disposal through an opening ship's bottom in approved disposal grounds down channel. *Glen Avon* got her name from the

Former Pill ferry ticket office.

Campbell steamer lost in the Second World War and was thus named at the launching ceremony in Troon by Mrs. (later Lady) Walker, wife of the then Leader of the City Council. The *Glen Avon*'s smart appearance belies her mundane role and her blue hull has been a familiar sight on the Avon for over 20 years.

On the starboard side we now pass Pill, the historic village that takes its name from the stream Crockerne Pill on which it stands. Pill is the traditional home of the Bristol Channel pilots, where the shelter of the pill was sufficiently close to the channel to allow the sailing pilot cutters swift access to the incoming ships that they sought to serve. The post-war years in Pill saw some sad decisions by the local planning committee when traditional cottages were replaced by quayside blocks of flats that went a long way to destroy the traditional charm of the place. Nowadays Crockerne Pill is the mooring place for many leisure craft which have taken the place of the pilot cutters of old.

Having passed Pill, our ship now enters Hung Road which in earlier years acted in the same capacity as a lorry park does now. Here ships would wait to discharge cargo into barges or simply sit out a tide if the journey to Bristol proved too long for safety. To avoid toppling when the ship took the ground as the water receded at low tide, the crew would rig a line from the ship's mast or side to the shore, and so 'hung' it. At the end of Hung Road, Chapel Pill enters the river on the starboard and it too has become an anchorage for small yachts.

On the port side the old Powder House now comes into view, overhanging the stream from its perch on a small cliff, reminding one of the days when ships going into Bristol off loaded their ammunition as a safety measure, and marking the start of the huge Horseshoe Bend. This bend is the limiting factor on the size of ships that can get up to Bristol and imposes a 300 feet overall length restriction. In earlier years the bend has claimed many victims, particularly in mist. The wartime perfection of radar as a navigation aid as well as a weapon has made the bend a much safer place but the post-war years have seen the occasional accident. The Campbell paddler *Glen Usk* went aground there on the north bank while outward bound with 600 passengers on the evening of August 30th 1959. No one was hurt and *Glen Usk* settled safely, to be pulled off the following morning by the tugs *Bristolian* and *John King*. On May 1st 1981, the motor excursion vessel *Prince Ivanhoe* struck the rocky south shore of the Horseshoe Bend inward bound and sustained enough damage to her bottom to cause her to spend two weeks in dry dock in Barry.

Once round the Horseshoe Bend, Sea Mills reach, a handsome stretch of water at high tide, lies ahead. On the north side the estuary of the River Trym was used in the eighteenth century as a dock to compete with Bristol, though not with any great commercial success. The Trym rises in north Bristol, as does its major tributary the Hen and both rivers provide the city with some of its most attractive scenery as they flow down to the Avon, particularly in the Blaise Castle estate. The Trym has a further purpose in today's scheme of things as it serves to drain surface storm water from the great housing estates of Southmead and Henbury which have sprung up since the war. Major flood relief schemes in Westbury village, where the Trym has been re-culverted, have removed the threat of the annual flooding of the village which was once a regular occurrence.

Soon after leaving Sea Mills the cliffs of the Avon Gorge come into sight, topped by the dramatic Clifton Suspension Bridge of I.K. Brunel and known world-wide as Bristol's trade mark. For drama of position and beauty of design and location it has few equals, rivalled only by the Golden Gate Bridge in San Francisco. Below, alongside the Portway, the relics of earlier days lie abandoned in the tunnels of the Port and Pier Railway and the bricked-up

The Trym at Westbury.

entrance to the Clifton Rocks Railway. To these sad reminders a new structure was added in the late seventies. Under the Suspension Bridge buttress, the 200 feet high limestone pillar which supports the north tower of the bridge, there was built an ugly concrete canopy to protect passing traffic from rock falling from the cliffs above. This hazard provided several near misses and large quantities of loose rock were removed from the gorge sides, particularly at Black Rock and the Sea Wall. The same remedy was obviously impossible at the Suspension Bridge site and hence the canopy was built by Avon County Council, the new traffic authority for Bristol. It is a telling reminder of the impact of motor traffic on the Bristol scene.

Ahead lies the start of the Floating Harbour: the entrance to Cumberland Basin, originally designed by Jessop and since improved by Brunel and others. But the Cumberland Basin postcard scene of tall ships passing has long gone and the most active post-war features are the swing bridges of the road scheme that carries traffic into the city from Bristol's dormitory towns south of the river. When the road scheme was built in the mid-sixties, care was taken to provide pedestrian routes, view points, cafés, kiosks and a transport cafe, in the belief that recreation and transient foot travellers could co-exist with the roar of the traffic above. This aspect of the scheme was a spectacular flop and today the cafés are closed and high uncut grass covers the view points. Incredibly, the whole scheme was designed in the City Engineer's office, which used Freeman Fox and Partners as consulting civil engineers. The Minister of Transport, Ernest Marples inaugurated the works on February 2nd 1963 with snow falling on the small crowd of workers, worthies and locals who had gathered for the event. Just over two years later the scheme had been completed and on April 14th 1965, the Transport Minister in the new Labour Government, Tom Fraser, arrived to open the new swing bridge which had been named appropriately after Bristol's Victorian M.P. and maritime reformer Samuel Plimsoll. After the usual speeches, the Minister pressed the button to swing the bridge which responded by sticking fast! It was to repeat the performance on other occasions, but none as embarrassing as that.

Here the river enters the Floating Harbour, the post-war history of which we have related in earlier chapters. Overflow water from that needed to maintain the harbour level by-passes the dock system by way of the New Cut and the two streams do not rejoin until the Avon resumes its journey above Netham Lock. In the harbour system, it has been joined by Colliters Brook and the Malago from the south and by the Frome from the north. All these streams have received attention from flood relief schemes in the post-war years. The capacity of the Malago to produce flash floods in South Bristol, as it did in

July 1968, led to the large Southern Interceptor Scheme. The Frome is Bristol's secret river, for while residents of Frenchay and Stapleton are familiar with the beauties of its valley, once it enters the city it winds a course largely hidden behind high buildings and which eventually vanishes underground to emerge in the city centre at St. Augustine's Reach. Here it provides a reminder of the 1247 diversion of the river to form the Quay. Upstream such names as Baptist Mills and Snuff Mills survive to remind one of industries long since abandoned.

At Netham Lock and weir, there are further reminders of change, most of it post-war. The tangle of factories that lined the Feeder Canal behind the lock, containing such industries as tanning, manure production and knackers' yards have largely gone, together with the unwholesome odour of their activities which used to foul the whole neighbourhood. On the skyline rise the tower blocks of the Council flats at Barton Hill, so admired at the time of their construction and now the subject of endless criticism. Landscaping has softened the scene but the incessant noise of motor traffic blights the area. Above, on the nearby railway bridge, the high speed trains of British Rail hurry to and from London on the world's fastest diesel-hauled service.

The Avon at Saltford.

77

Above Netham, as the Avon prepares to enter Bristol, there is no escape from industrial dereliction. On the south bank the remains of St. Anne's Board Mills, which closed in 1979, have been partially redeveloped but still await the implementation of plans for the area. On the other bank, the tar distillery at Crews Hole was closed and then levelled in 1981. The hillside above Crews Hole was used by Bristol City Council as a rubbish tip in the early sixties, something they would never get away with today. By the time the author became Chairman of the Public Works Committee at the end of 1967, the tipping had been completed and the tip 'stabilised'. Late one evening in mid-1968, the author was telephoned by a member of the City Engineer's Department to say they suspected the tip was moving downhill and several thousand tons of untreated rubbish was on its way into the Avon! As events turned out, this alarm was something of an exaggeration. The tip was moving but only about two inches every 24 hours and it was possible to build up the foot with hardcore and thus hold it in place. Today, twenty years on it has merged into the scenery at Crews Hole. Now, the tall chimney on the crest of Troopers Hill is the last reminder of the industry that littered the valley.

Now the scene changes as one goes up-stream round St. Anne's and the woods of Conham Vale, Hencliff Wood and Fox's Wood come into view. Here the river adopts a rural, verdant calm that for a mile or so rivals anything the Wye has to offer. As Hanham Mills are reached, the tidal range of the Avon is finally exhausted, 14½ miles from the sea.

When one has exhausted the delights of the Chequers Inn at Hanham Weir, the course upstream to Bath is one of the most pleasant stretches of water in England. Past green river meadows where gaps in the bank seem to be perpetually occupied by fishermen, the river passes Frys Chocolate Factory, rises through Keynsham Lock and its nearby marina and then carries on to Bitton. Keynsham still retains memories of the 1968 floods when the County Bridge was a victim of the torrent. At Bitton there is a chance to visit Bitton Station and the preserved steam trains of the Avon Valley Railway, which celebrated 21 years of operation in 1992. After Swineford, the river valley opens up and goes past Saltford on the last stages of its run up to Bath.

The Kennet and Avon Canal, like most transport systems, came into being piecemeal, the first parts being proposed in a Bill of 1708, which opened up the Kennet at the Reading end, although Royal Assent was not obtained until 1715 and work not completed until 1724. The Avon was opened up between Hanham and Bath by 1727 but not until 1794 was a bill moved which allowed the two systems to be joined. Sixteen years later the canal opened, one year after Bristol's new Floating Harbour.

Pulteney Bridge, Bath.

Success was to be short lived as the Great Western Railway had its London-Bath-Bristol line in operation by 1841 and canals were in decline. By 1852, the GWR had acquired all the assets of the Kennet and Avon company, on the understanding that the canal was kept open. This the GWR valiantly did for the next century, until in the 1950s the canal works were in sad shape. Navigation over the whole length became impossible. Then, in a determined and eventually triumphant restoration campaign, the Kennet and Avon Canal Trust resurrected the canal until the great day when it was re-opened by Queen Elizabeth II. A flight of locks in Bath, Nos 7 to 13, among which is the deepest canal lock in the country, introduces the boat owner to the canal and allows access to a waterborne system that connects Bristol to the Thames and eventually to London. It is surely one of Britain's and Bristol's post-war triumphs.

Towards the year 2000

"And a star shone over Bristol, wonderfully far
and high."

John Betjeman.

The Port of Bristol passed from private into public ownership with the passage of the Bristol Dock Act, 1848. On July 30th of that year the responsibility for the port passed to the City Council and its Docks Committee. For 153 years the committee ran the port in good times and bad but as the 1990s dawned, it became more obvious than ever that radical change was needed if the port was to survive into the 21st century. The 1980s had been years of drastic changes in the port industry, as in many others. The corporatism of the middle century had been discarded as a viable economic system by all but a few and the nation took Margaret Thatcher's privatisation programmes in its stride. The major change in port activities was the abolition of the National Dock Labour Scheme. When introduced the scheme had the worthy aim of protecting dockers' pay and conditions but it grew into a monstrous labyrinth of restrictive practices that held up port development and growth. The Port of Bristol stuck doggedly to its terms for another year but then accepted the inevitable.

Another sign of the changing times were defence expenditure reductions which led to the withdrawal from service of H.M.S. *Bristol*, the Type 82 destroyer built on the Tyne. The veteran warship, which served in the Falklands task force in 1982, made her last visit to Avonmouth in early June 1991 and was decommissioned at Portsmouth on the 27th of that month in a ceremony attended by many of her previous commanding officers.

The last years of the eighties had also brought difficulties for the City Council on another front, that of planning and development. This was to have a direct consequence for the waterway system at the centre of the city. The mid-eighties had seen an increasingly acrimonious debate between the city planners and private sector architects, estate agents and developers. This centred around the alleged difficulties that were experienced in obtaining planning permissions in the city compared with like cities elsewhere. This led the professions in the city to publish a report in late 1985 called 'Planning

H.M.S. *Bristol*.

Difficulties in Bristol'. This in turn led to a public row which was never really resolved and, if it had been an isolated incident, would have been soon forgotten. But immediately in its wake came the news that Lloyds Bank had chosen Canon's Marsh as the preferred site of a large new banking complex, a proposal that drove a coach and horses through current city planning policy for the area. For years, the Canon's Marsh planning brief had clearly kept office development out of proposals for the site and most commentators saw the granting of permission as a complete U-turn.

Behind the decision, in the opinion of many, was the City Council's desire to avoid an urban development corporation being set up in Bristol. These autonomous independent planning authorities were a product of the Conservative government's impatience with the slow pace, as they saw it, of urban renewal in Britain's city centres. The development corporations were given considerable powers and finance to get on with the job. The first batch included such well known areas of dereliction as the London docklands and the programme got a further boost when Mrs. Thatcher won the 1987 General Election. After the row over planning difficulties in Bristol, there was an even chance that the city would feature in a future list of new development corporations. So it proved when on December 7th 1987 the setting up of the Bristol Development Corporation was announced. Its designated area was to be all that land that lay around the River Avon and the Feeder Canal, east from Temple Meads Station to the city boundary at St. Anne's.

Our purpose here is to look at the impact of the setting up of the BDC on the city's waterways but it must be recorded in passing that the decision triggered off an angry response from the City Council. Other provincial cities which have been designated development corporations have, almost without exception, co-operated with the new bodies to the benefit of both authorities, but Bristol at the outset decided not to do so.

The Lloyds Bank headquarters building in Canon's Marsh.

Open warfare has been relieved by one glowing exception: the BDC's proposal for the Avon Weir. The BDC has, in all its proposals, taken account of the importance of the city's waterways to amenity and environment, particularly in the plans for Temple Meads and St. Anne's Board Mills. The building of a weir at Gaol Ferry Bridge, well down the New Cut from Temple Meads, would have the effect of transforming the present tidal mud flats of the Avon and New Cut into a recreational amenity which would give constant water level and improve the appearance of the river. The design of the weir by Sir Alexander Gibb and Partners has a flap gate along its crest to enable control of the water level, while a sluice enables control of flood water. At the moment, the river below Netham Dam is tidal with large amounts of accumulated

The entrance to Watershed, with the refurbished and extended Swallow Royal Hotel.

rubbish on view between tides. The weir project should change this depressing scene for the better. The initial cost has been estimated at £10 million, much of which could be recovered through contributions from bankside developers. A Bill was introduced into Parliament in November 1990, with the aim of completing construction by the end of 1994.

In parallel with the Avon Weir scheme, several private proposals for development along the river system have emerged in recent years. By far the most imaginative was the proposal by Bristol architect Angus Macdonald for a series of multi-purpose buildings suspended on crossings of the New Cut. Lower down the river, just below the M5 Bridge is the site proposed by a consortium led by Bolton Estates for an Avon barrage which would include a 200 metre × 15 metre lock to allow shipping to continue to go up to Bristol, and also carry a two-lane highway and railway line across the Avon.

While the battles between the Council and the BDC raged upriver, at Avonmouth 1991 saw the city authorities take a positive and historic decision on the future of the Port of Bristol. Since re-organisation of local government in 1974 and the establishment of Avon County Council, the City Council had battled, as we have seen, with increasing financial difficulties over port operations. At one stage, merchant bankers working for Arab clients had been approached to construct an investment scheme but without success. Almost two decades passed and then in late 1989 the city received an approach from the directors of First Corporate Shipping who were anxious to mount a bid for the port business. It was an act of considerable courage and realism by the ruling Labour Group to go ahead with a negotiation which was certainly against long held views on municipal ownership. After a year long series of talks, agreement was reached. In a £25 million deal, Avonmouth and Portbury docks were placed on long lease to First Corporate Shipping and the port passed out of municipal control after 153 years. First Corporate were led by their directors Terence Mordaunt and David Ord, and Dr. Douglas Naysmith, the Port Chairman, and Robert Trench, a previous holder of the office, were prominent among the council team.

First Corporate traded at Bristol under the title The Bristol Port Company and in the first year of operations achieved remarkable success. Work started on a new £70 million bulk terminal that was planned to open in 1993 with a capacity for handling 10 million tonnes of cargo annually. The port also won considerable car import contracts and handlings in 1992 were expected to exceed 60,000. Flexible working practices were introduced and the port once again began to recruit labour. New management and the invigorating approach of the private sector was well on its way to restoring the Port of Bristol to the top rank of British ports, and ensuring that it would go into the 21st century in a fit condition to endure.

Meanwhile other pressures were ensuring further developments in the Avonmouth area, which would promise well for the future. The Government claim, and who can disbelieve them, that the Severn Bridge has carried over 275 million vehicles since it opened in 1966. Between 1980 and 1990, traffic increased by 63% and the M4 and M5 motorways were threatened with saturation at peak periods as the figures were predicted to go even higher. As early as 1986, the Department of Transport announced the intention to construct a second Severn crossing at the English Stones, some three miles downstream from the present bridge. After much preparatory work, a Bill was introduced into Parliament in November 1990 to obtain the necessary powers. A policy decision ensured that the second crossing would be built by the private sector and a company was formed, Severn River Crossing plc, which was a consortium of John Laing plc and the French firm GTM Entrepose Joint Venture which would design, finance and build the whole project. The total cost was estimated to be over £200 million.

The second Severn crossing will span the estuary from the shore south-east of Caldicot to a spot on the English side between Severn Beach and the New Passage. Here the deep water channel runs on the Welsh side of the estuary at an area known as The Shoots. Here, in order to accommodate shipping movements, there will be a cable stayed bridge which will span 456 metres and give a high water clearance of 37 metres on spring tides. The overall length of the bridge will be 912 metres. Road viaducts will connect the two shores to the bridge. There will be a three lane highway in each direction with a toll booth area on the Welsh side. Tolls will be collected in a westward direction only on both bridges and the whole project will be financed from income generated by both bridges. Exploratory work on the river bed started in 1991 and foundation stones were laid by the Secretary of State for Transport, John MacGregor and Secretary of State for Wales, David Hunt on September 14th 1992. When completed and open to traffic by the target date of early 1996, the scheme will be one to rival the Bay Bridges complex at San Francisco.

For the Severnside town of Avonmouth (for such it is) and for the villages of Pilning, Severn Beach and Redwick the construction of the bridge must be regarded as a mixed blessing. They will suffer disruption caused by the construction works and continuous traffic noise, although so-called amenity mounds of earthworks are proposed to protect residential areas from traffic noise. On the positive side must be placed the development opportunities and enhanced land values that will come in the wake of the new roads that are being

Looking ahead to the Tall Ships Race, 1997: the *Christian Radich*.

constructed to integrate the new crossing with the Severn Bridge and existing motorways. Already in 1991, as an example, a proposal was announced for the construction of a large gas-fired electrical power generating station on Severnside. It was likely to be only the first major scheme in the economic development of an area which stands at the junction of two motorways and a mainline railway which gives access within two hours to two-thirds of the population of England and Wales. The main markets of the EEC lie only a twelve hour journey away at the most. This geographical position alone puts Bristol and its port in a position to make the 21st century yet another period of growth if the opportunities are recognised and exploited.

In all these plans for the Port of Bristol and its hinterland, two issues remained to be resolved. The first was relatively straightforward: the modernisation of the West country's main railway lines with the installation of electric traction. By the mid-nineties the popular and effective high speed diesel powered HST 125s would all be coming to the later part of their working life and the question of a suitable replacement system was long overdue for consideration. Successful electrification of the east coast main line to Scotland and the proposed Heathrow link make it clear that electrification of the west routes is only a matter of time.

The other unresolved question was the site for Bristol's international air route terminus. Air travel, despite the recession of the early nineties, is forecast to grow steadily again by the end of the decade and both the municipal airport at Lulsgate and the British Aerospace airfield at Filton have plans for future expansion. The proposals of both fields have attracted considerable public opposition for amenity reasons but the decision will have to be made in the not-too-distant future.

Not so critical to Bristol's future but certain to have an impact, if eventually constructed, is the Severn Barrage, a proposal of long standing that has been argued with greater or lesser enthusiasm over the post-war years, although the idea first surfaced before the war. The scheme that emerged from Government studies in the 1980s envisaged a barrage crossing the Bristol Channel from Brean Down, two miles downstream from Weston-super-Mare, to Lavernock Point, between Penarth and Barry in South Glamorgan. A series of huge sluices would harness the Severn tidal rise to activate turbine driven power generation. There would be locks on the Welsh side, where the deep channel lies, to let ocean going shipping up to Cardiff, Newport, Bristol and Gloucester. A motor highway was planned to travel along the top of the barrage to connect Somerset and Glamorgan. Salmon ladders were planned into the proposals to protect the world famous fisheries on the Wye and the

Severn. Authorities differed on the impact that the barrage would have on the ecology of the Channel and there were even differing views of the total contribution that the generators would make to the National Grid.

The Government made it quite clear that it was in no hurry to proceed with the scheme and when it did give the go ahead, it would expect the huge construction costs to be carried by the private sector. There were few around as the nineties dawned in an atmosphere of depression able to contemplate the investment of such huge sums in a project that had yet to be fully designed. The 21st century is likely to be several decades old before the Severn Barrage becomes reality.

In 1997 the City of Bristol will celebrate the 500th anniversary of the voyage of John Cabot from the city to discover the mainland of North America. The full story of the Cabot voyage has been told, as far as it is known, in the author's earlier volume *Bristol: Maritime City* (Redcliffe Press 1981) but a short résumé is appropriate here.

John Cabot came to Bristol from Genoa via Venice and settled here sometime in the 1490s. He made an impact in the city, securing letters patent from King Henry VII on March 5th 1496 to, inter alia, 'sail to all parts, countries and seas of the east, of the west, and of the north . . . and find whatsoever isles, countries, regions, or provinces of the heathens and infidels whatsoever they be . . .' Cabot left Bristol on May 2nd 1497 in the *Matthew* of 50 tons and, after 35 days of voyaging in mostly fair weather, sighted land on the feast of St. John, June 24th. There is no evidence to pinpoint the landing place and it could be anywhere from Labrador to Maine. Newfoundland is the popular choice of historians. The *Matthew* returned to Bristol and a great welcome on August 6th and Cabot's name went into the history books.

In 1997, half a millenium later, joint celebrations are planned in Bristol and Newfoundland. The anniversary is a great opportunity to present Bristol to the world. There will be events and exhibitions on both sides of the Atlantic but the highlight of the occasion will be the voyage from Bristol of a full scale replica of the *Matthew*. In 1991, Bristol Cabot 500 committee was formed under the auspices of the Bristol Initiative and chaired by St. John Hartnell, senior partner of Hartnell, Taylor and Cook and a well known and popular Bristol figure. The intention is to build the ship in Bristol to plans as near as can be schemed of a late fifteenth century ship, as no known plans of the original *Matthew* exist.

So, as the Port of Bristol prepares to celebrate the most famous voyage ever made from its quays, it has taken new life from the post-war years and is poised in the 21st century to see some of its most prosperous and exciting times.

Major opportunities are beginning to appear once more. Placed on the Atlantic seaboard of the EEC, but only a short distance by Channel Tunnel or ferry to the major centres of the single market, the city has some of the greatest investment prospects in Europe if its public bodies put dissent behind them. The people of Bristol need only have faith in themselves and their ability to overcome difficulties – and the vision to seek out new fields of enterprise – to make the voyage of the second *Matthew* in 1997 open up gateways to new worlds of enterprise and opportunity.

The replica Cabot's *Matthew*, as she might look.

Bibliography

Allsop, Niall *Images of The Kennet & Avon Canal* (Bristol 1987)*
Baker, Robert *Avon Voyage* (Bath 1982)
Belsey et al. *Bristol in the Fifties* (Bristol 1988)*
Coombes, Nigel *Passenger Steamers of the Bristol Channel*
Farr, Graham *West Country Passenger Steamers* (Prescot 1967)
Farr, Graham *Wreck & Rescue in the Bristol Channel* (Truro 1966)
Goold-Adams, Richard *The Return of the Great Britain* (London 1976)
Hill, John C.G. *Shipshape & Bristol Fashion* (2nd Bristol 1983)*
Holyoak, Jon *Balmoral* (Glasgow 1986)
Langham, A. & M. *Lundy* (Newton Abbott 1970)
Lord & Southam *The Floating Harbour* (Bristol 1983)*
Little, Bryan *The City and County of Bristol* (London 1954)
Little, Bryan *John Cabot: The Reality* (Bristol 1983)*
Punter, John V. *Design Control in Bristol 1940–1990* (Bristol 1990)*
Manson, Michael *Bristol beyond the Bridge* (Bristol 1988)*
Shipsides & Wall *Bristol – Maritime City* (Bristol 1981)*
Wall, Robert *Bristol Channel Pleasure Steamers* (Newton Abbott 1973)
Winstone, Reece *Bristol As It Was* (37 vols. Private various dates)

Sources – Newspapers, Records & Archives

Files of *Bristol Evening Post*, *Bristol Evening World* and *Western Daily Press*.
City Archives of the City of Bristol.
Minutes of the City Council 1945–1992.
Minutes of the Docks Committee (Port of Bristol Authority).

* Published by Redcliffe Press.

Index

95